Quick & Easy
Puddings

p

Contents

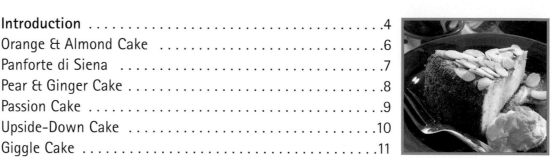

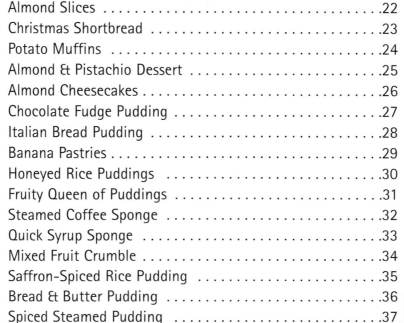

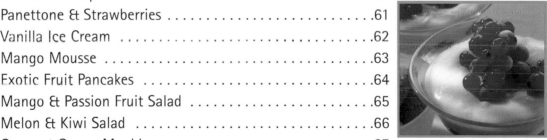

Introduction

For anyone with a sweet tooth no meal is complete without a sumptuous pudding to finish it off. Desserts come in a multitude of forms, and everyone has their favourite — whether it be the taste of Italy in a Tiramisu, a taste of the Orient in an exotic fruit salad or a Traditional American Apple Pie, all tastes have been catered for in *Puddings*.

A Historical Role

Puddings have enjoyed pride of place on the table through history, around the world. From rich chocolate desserts which followed the arrival and widespread use of the cocoa bean in western Europe in the eighteenth century, to beautifully simple yet delicious fruit salads made from the fresh fruit of local trees, a dessert is always something special. Puddings have always held an individual place in a meal, they signify a luxury — even in the richest of households. Traditionally the pudding arrives at the end of the meal when people can barely eat any more, yet most manage to eat their share of the *pièce de résistance*, which may be served with

much pomp and ceremony. Ornate dishes, decorative tableware and the best cutlery are frequently reserved for serving this part of the meal. A successful pudding is one of which to be very proud.

Spoil Yourself!

Puddings are a real opportunity to spoil the gourmand in you. You can impress family and friends, make tempting treats for special occasions, birthdays or dinner parties — or simply spoil yourself. With very little effort you can create stunning masterpieces that decorate a table as well as providing a delicious end to a meal.

Healthy Eating

For those who crave a warm winter pudding or a summer trifle without piling on the calories, recipes have been found that the health-conscious can enjoy. Fruit is an excellent ingredient for low-fat puddings as it is fat-free and naturally sweet. The huge

variety of fruit available in supermarkets and green-grocers means that many different flavours and textures can be achieved.

Vegetarian

Vegetarians can enjoy a wealth of dishes from the dessert menu although strict vegetarians should avoid puddings that contain gelatin. From rich chocolate fudge puddings and fruit crumbles, to bread and butter puddings and passion cake, there really are so many different choices!

Family Favourites

Puddings contains selections of all of your favourite desserts: cakes and gateaux, small cakes and biscuits, hot and cold puddings. A sumptuous treat can be found for any time of day or year. All of the family's favourites have been included from Coconut Sweet, ideal for children's parties and packed lunches, to the traditional Upside-Down Cake — a real afternoon treat. Among these irresistible puddings are some new adaptations of old tea-time favourites.

Cooking Times and Techniques

Some puddings may take a while to prepare, others may need to spend time in the oven to cook and others still will need to be left to cool or stand before serving. Make sure you read the recipe through when planning

your meal. Despite the fact that the pudding is probably the last dish to arrive on your table, it may be best to prepare it, or begin cooking it first. And remember, all ovens do vary so alter cooking times in accordance with your oven and keep checking the progress of the dessert when possible.

The following terms are common in dessert recipes and these definitions will help you achieve the best results:

Blending: Involves the mixing together of two or more ingredients with a spoon, beater or electric blender until they are completely combined.

Folding: Used to carefully combine light, airy ingredients (such as egg whites) with heavier mixtures (such as cream) without losing too much of the air contained in the lighter one. Folding is a delicate technique where the lighter mixture is placed on top of the heavier one in a bowl sufficiently large to incorporate all the ingredients, with enough room to mix. A rubber spatula must be used to fold ingredients and the mixing should be done slowly and carefully. Cutting down through the mixture from the back of the bowl towards the front

and lifting the bottom mixture over the top, whilst turning the bowl a quarter turn after each stroke, is the best method of folding ingredients together. Continue until the two different mixtures are fully combined.

Creaming: Used to combine ingredients until they are smooth and 'creamy' in texture. Fat and butter are two ingredients which are frequently combined in this way. The ingredients are creamed when you can no longer see the different constituents and they have formed a homogenous paste; electric mixers can greatly speed up this process.

Greasing: Essential in baking to stop ingredients from sticking to their containers during cooking. Butter is ideal for greasing cake tins or baking trays. Use greaseproof paper or butter wrappers covered in fat to rub the base and sides of the tray or pan, leaving a thin coating of grease. If asked to grease and flour the container, apply the grease and then sprinkle flour over the top. Shake the container to ensure a complete and even cover and then tip the pan or tray upside down over the sink to remove any excess flour.

Beating: The most common way to mix ingredients, it simply means combining all the ingredients using a spoon, fork or mixer by stirring rapidly in a circular motion. Electric mixers save a lot of time and energy and are much better than beating ingredients by hand.

How to Make the Best Puddings

- Start by reading the recipe all the way through.
- Weigh all the ingredients accurately and do basic preparation, such as grating and chopping, before you start cooking.
- Basic cake-making ingredients should be kept at room temperature.
- Mixtures that are creamed should be almost white and have a 'soft dropping' consistency. This can be done by hand, but using a hand-held electric mixer will save time.
- Do not remove a cake from the oven until it is fully cooked. To test if a cake is cooked, press the surface lightly with your fingertips – it should feel springy to the touch. Alternatively, insert a fine metal skewer into the centre of the cake – it will come out clean if the cake is cooked through.
- Leave cakes in their tins to cool before carefully turning out on to a wire rack to cool completely.

KEY

 Simplicity level 1 – 3 (1 easiest, 3 slightly harder)

 Preparation time

 Cooking time

Orange & Almond Cake

This light and tangy citrus cake from Sicily is better eaten as a dessert than as a cake. It is especially good served after a large meal.

NUTRITIONAL INFORMATION

Calories	399	Sugars	........20g
Protein	.........8g	Fat	..........31g
Carbohydrate	...23g	Saturates	......13g

 30 MINS   40 MINS

SERVES 8

INGREDIENTS

4 eggs, separated

125 g/4½ oz caster (superfine) sugar, plus
2 tsp for the cream

finely grated rind and juice of 2 oranges

finely grated rind and juice of 1 lemon

125 g/4½ oz ground almonds

25 g/1 oz self-raising flour

200 ml/7 fl oz/¾ cup whipping (light) cream

1 tsp cinnamon

25 g/1 oz flaked (slivered) almonds, toasted

icing (confectioners') sugar, to dust

1 Grease and line the base of a 18 cm/ 7 inch round deep cake tin (pan).

2 Blend the egg yolks with the sugar until the mixture is thick and creamy. Whisk half of the orange rind and all of the lemon rind into the egg yolks.

VARIATION

You could serve this cake with a syrup. Boil the juice and finely grated rind of 2 oranges, 75 g/2¾ oz caster (superfine) sugar and 2 tbsp of water for 5–6 minutes until slightly thickened. Stir in 1 tbsp of orange liqueur just before serving.

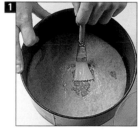  

3 Mix the juice from both oranges and the lemon with the ground almonds and stir into the egg yolks. The mixture will become quite runny at this point. Fold in the flour.

4 Whisk the egg whites until stiff and gently fold into the egg yolk mixture.

5 Pour the mixture into the tin (pan) and bake in a preheated oven, at 180°C/350°F/Gas Mark 4, for 35–40 minutes, or until golden and springy to the touch. Leave to cool in the tin (pan) for 10 minutes and then turn out. It is likely to sink slightly at this stage.

6 Whip the cream to form soft peaks. Stir in the remaining orange rind, cinnamon and sugar.

7 Once the cake is cold, cover with the almonds, dust with icing (confectioners') sugar and serve with the cream.

Panforte di Siena

This famous Tuscan honey and nut cake is a Christmas speciality. In Italy it is sold in pretty boxes, and served in very thin slices.

NUTRITIONAL INFORMATION

Calories ....257 Sugars 29g
Protein ....5g Fat 13g
Carbohydrate ...33g Saturates 1g

 10 MINS 1¼ HOURS

SERVES 12

I N G R E D I E N T S

125 g/4½ oz/1 cup split whole almonds

125 g/4½ oz/¾ cup hazelnuts

90 g/3 oz/½ cup cut mixed peel

60 g/2 oz/⅓ cup no-soak dried apricots

60 g/2 oz glacé or crystallized pineapple

grated rind of 1 large orange

60 g/2 oz/½ cup plain (all-purpose) flour

2 tbsp cocoa powder

2 tsp ground cinnamon

125 g/4½ oz/½ cup caster (superfine) sugar

175 g/6 oz/½ cup honey

icing (confectioners') sugar, for dredging

1 Toast the almonds under the grill (broiler) until lightly browned and place in a bowl.

2 Toast the hazelnuts until the skins split. Place on a dry tea towel (dish cloth) and rub off the skins. Roughly chop the hazelnuts and add to the almonds with the mixed peel.

3 Chop the apricots and pineapple fairly finely, add to the nuts with the orange rind and mix well.

4 Sift the flour with the cocoa and cinnamon, add to the nut mixture; mix.

5 Line a round 20 cm/8 inch cake tin or deep loose-based flan tin (pan) with baking parchment.

6 Put the sugar and honey into a saucepan and heat until the sugar dissolves, then boil gently for about 5 minutes or until the mixture thickens and begins to turn a deeper shade of brown. Quickly add to the nut mixture and mix evenly. Turn into the prepared tin (pan) and level the top using the back of a damp spoon.

7 Cook in a preheated oven, at 150°C/ 300°F/Gas Mark 2, for 1 hour. Remove from the oven and leave in the tin (pan) until cold. Take out of the tin (pan) and carefully peel off the paper. Before serving, dredge the cake heavily with sifted icing (confectioners') sugar. Serve in very thin slices.

Pear & Ginger Cake

This deliciously buttery pear and ginger cake is ideal for tea-time or you can serve it with cream for a delicious dessert.

NUTRITIONAL INFORMATION

Calories 531	Sugars 41g
Protein 6g	Fat 30g
Carbohydrate . . .62g	Saturates 19g

 15 MINS   40 MINS

SERVES 6

INGREDIENTS

200 g/7 oz/14 tbsp unsalted butter, softened

175 g/6 oz caster (superfine) sugar

175 g/6 oz self-raising flour, sifted

3 tsp ginger

3 eggs, beaten

450 g/1 lb dessert (eating) pears, peeled, cored and thinly sliced

1 tbsp soft brown sugar

1 Lightly grease and line the base of a deep 20.5 cm/8 inch cake tin (pan).

2 Using a whisk, combine 175 g/6 oz of the butter with the sugar, flour, ginger and eggs and mix to form a smooth consistency.

3 Spoon the cake mixture into the prepared tin (pan), levelling out the surface.

4 Arrange the pear slices over the cake mixture. Sprinkle with the brown sugar and dot with the remaining butter.

5 Bake in a preheated oven, at 180°C/350°F/Gas Mark 4, for 35–40 minutes or until the cake is golden and feels springy to the touch.

6 Serve the pear and ginger cake warm, with ice cream or cream, if you wish.

COOK'S TIP

Soft, brown sugar is often known as Barbados sugar. It is a darker form of light brown soft sugar.

Passion Cake

Decorating this moist, rich carrot cake with sugared flowers lifts it into the celebration class. It is a perfect choice for Easter.

NUTRITIONAL INFORMATION

Calories 506	Sugars 40g	
Protein 10g	Fat 27g	
Carbohydrate ...60g	Saturates 4g	

15 MINS   1½ HOURS

SERVES 10

I N G R E D I E N T S

150 ml/¼ pint/⅔ cup corn oil

175 g/6 oz/¾ cup golden caster (superfine) sugar

4 tbsp natural (unsweetened) yogurt

3 eggs, plus 1 extra yolk

1 tsp vanilla essence (extract)

125 g/4½ oz/1 cup walnut pieces, chopped

175 g/6 oz carrots, grated

1 banana, mashed

175 g/6 oz/1½ cups plain (all-purpose) flour

90 g/3 oz/½ cup fine oatmeal

1 tsp bicarbonate of soda (baking soda)

1 tsp baking powder

1 tsp ground cinnamon

½ tsp salt

I C I N G   (F R O S T I N G)

150 g/5½ oz/generous ½ cup soft cheese

4 tbsp natural (unsweetened) yogurt

90 g/3 oz/¾ cup icing (confectioners') sugar

1 tsp grated lemon rind

2 tsp lemon juice

D E C O R A T I O N

primroses and violets

1 egg white, lightly beaten

40 g/1½ oz/3 tbsp caster (superfine) sugar

1 Grease and line a 23 cm/9 inch round cake tin (pan). Beat together the oil, sugar, yogurt, eggs, egg yolk and vanilla essence (extract). Beat in the chopped walnuts, grated carrot and banana.

2 Sift together the remaining ingredients and gradually beat into the mixture.

3 Pour the mixture into the tin (pan) and level the surface. Bake in a preheated oven, 180°C/350°F/Gas Mark 4, for 1½ hours, or until firm. To test, insert a fine skewer into the centre: it should come out clean. Leave to cool in the tin (pan) for 15 minutes, then turn out on to a wire rack.

4 To make the frosting, beat together the cheese and yogurt. Sift in the icing (confectioners') sugar and stir in the lemon rind and juice. Spread over the top and sides of the cake.

5 To prepare the decoration, dip the flowers quickly in the beaten egg white, then sprinkle with caster (superfine) sugar to cover the surface completely. Place well apart on baking parchment. Leave in a warm, dry place for several hours until they are dry and crisp. Arrange the flowers in a pattern on top of the cake.

Upside-Down Cake

This recipe shows how a classic favourite can be adapted for vegans by using vegetarian margarine and oil instead of butter and eggs.

NUTRITIONAL INFORMATION

Calories	354	Sugars	........31g
Protein	.........3g	Fat	..........15g
Carbohydrate	...56g	Saturates	.......2g

15 MINS   50 MINS

SERVES 6

INGREDIENTS

50 g/1¾ oz/¼ cup vegan margarine,
  cut into small pieces, plus extra
  for greasing

425 g/15 oz can unsweetened pineapple
  pieces, drained and juice reserved

4 tsp cornflour (cornstarch)

50 g/1¾ oz/¼ cup soft brown sugar

125 ml/4 fl oz/½ cup water

rind of 1 lemon

SPONGE

50 ml/2 fl oz/¼ cup sunflower oil

75 g/2¾ oz/⅓ cup soft brown sugar

150 ml/¼ pint/⅔ cup water

150 g/5½ oz/1¼ cups plain
  (all-purpose) flour

2 tsp baking powder

1 tsp ground cinnamon

1 Grease a deep 18 cm/7 inch cake tin (pan). Mix the reserved juice from the pineapple with the cornflour (cornstarch) until it forms a smooth paste. Put the paste in a saucepan with the sugar, margarine and water and stir over a low heat until the sugar has dissolved. Bring to the boil and simmer for 2–3 minutes, until thickened. Set aside to cool slightly.

2 To make the sponge, place the oil, sugar and water in a saucepan. Heat gently until the sugar has dissolved; do not allow it to boil. Remove from the heat and leave to cool. Sift the flour, baking powder and ground cinnamon into a mixing bowl. Pour over the cooled sugar syrup and beat well to form a batter.

3 Place the pineapple pieces and lemon rind on the base of the prepared tin (pan) and pour over 4 tablespoons of the pineapple syrup. Spoon the sponge batter on top.

4 Bake in a preheated oven, 180°C/350°F/Gas Mark 4, for 35–40 minutes, until set and a fine metal skewer inserted into the centre comes out clean. Invert on to a plate, leave to stand for 5 minutes, then remove the tin (pan). Serve with the remaining syrup.

Giggle Cake

It's a mystery how this cake got its name – perhaps it's because it's easy to make and fun to eat.

NUTRITIONAL INFORMATION

Calories	493	Sugars	........66g
Protein	.........6g	Fat	..........15g
Carbohydrate	...90g	Saturates	.......3g

 25 MINS 1¼ HOURS

SERVES 8

INGREDIENTS

350 g/12 oz/2 cups mixed dried fruit

125 g/4½ oz/½ cup butter or margarine

175 g/6 oz/1 cup soft brown sugar

225 g/8 oz/2 cups self-raising (self-rising) flour

pinch of salt

2 eggs, beaten

225 g/8 oz can chopped pineapple, drained

125 g/4½ oz/½ cup glacé (candied) cherries, halved

1 Put the mixed dried fruit into a large bowl and cover with boiling water. Set aside to soak for 10–15 minutes, then drain well.

2 Put the butter or margarine and sugar into a large saucepan and heat gently until melted. Add the drained mixed dried fruit and cook over a low heat, stirring frequently, for 4–5 minutes. Remove from the heat and transfer to a mixing bowl. Set aside to cool.

3 Sift together the flour and salt into the dried fruit mixture and stir well. Add the eggs, mixing until the ingredients are thoroughly incorporated.

4 Add the pineapples and cherries to the cake mixture and stir to combine. Transfer to a greased and lined 1 kg/2 lb loaf tin (pan) and level the surface.

5 Bake in a preheated oven, 180°C/ 350°F/Gas Mark 4, for about 1 hour. Test the cake with a fine skewer; if it comes out clean, the cake is cooked. If not, return to the oven for a few more minutes. Cool and serve.

VARIATION

If you wish, add 1 teaspoon ground mixed spice (apple spice) to the cake mixture, sifting it in with the flour. Bake the cake in an 18 cm/7 inch round cake tin (pan) if you don't have a loaf tin (pan) of the right size. Remember to grease and line it first.

Carrot & Ginger Cake

This melt-in-the-mouth version of a favourite cake has a fraction of the fat of the traditional cake.

NUTRITIONAL INFORMATION

Calories 249	Sugars 28g	
Protein 7g	Fat 6g	
Carbohydrate ...46g	Saturates 1g	

15 MINS   1¼ HOURS

SERVES 10

INGREDIENTS

225 g/8 oz plain (all-purpose) flour

1 tsp baking powder

1 tsp bicarbonate of soda

2 tsp ground ginger

½ tsp salt

175 g/6 oz light muscovado sugar

225 g/8 oz carrots, grated

2 pieces stem ginger in syrup, drained and chopped

25 g/1 oz root (fresh) ginger, grated

60 g/2 oz seedless raisins

2 medium eggs, beaten

3 tbsp corn oil

juice of 1 medium orange

ICING (FROSTING)

225 g/8 oz low-fat soft cheese

4 tbsp icing (confectioners') sugar

1 tsp vanilla essence (extract)

TO DECORATE

grated carrot

stem (fresh) ginger

ground ginger

1 Preheat the oven to 180°C/350°F/Gas Mark 4. Grease and line a 20.5 cm/8 inch round cake tin with baking parchment.

2 Sift the flour, baking powder, bicarbonate of soda, ground ginger and salt into a bowl. Stir in the sugar, carrots, stem ginger, root (fresh) ginger and raisins. Beat together the eggs, oil and orange juice, then pour into the bowl. Mix the ingredients together well.

3 Spoon the mixture into the tin and bake in the oven for 1–1¼ hours until firm to the touch, or until a skewer

inserted into the centre of the cake comes out clean.

4 To make the frosting, place the soft cheese in a bowl and beat to soften. Sift in the icing (confectioners') sugar and add the vanilla essence (extract). Mix well.

5 Remove the cake from the tin (pan) and smooth the frosting over the top. Decorate the cake and serve.

Tofu (Bean Curd) Cake

This cake has a rich creamy texture just like cheesecake, but contains no dairy produce. With crushed biscuits it is easy to make a 'pastry' case.

NUTRITIONAL INFORMATION

Calories 282   Sugars 17g
Protein . . . . .9g   Fat 15g
Carbohydrate . . .29g   Saturates 4g

 10 MINS   45 MINS

SERVES 4

INGREDIENTS

125 g/4½ oz low-fat digestive biscuits (graham crackers), crushed

50 g/1¾ oz/10 tsp margarine, melted

50 g/1¾ oz stoned dates, chopped

4 tbsp lemon juice

rind of 1 lemon

3 tbsp water

350 g/12 oz packet firm tofu (bean curd)

150 ml/¼ pint/⅔ cup apple juice

1 banana, mashed

1 tsp vanilla flavouring (extract)

1 mango, peeled and chopped

1 Lightly grease an 18 cm/7 inch round loose-bottomed cake tin (pan).

2 Mix together the digestive biscuit (graham cracker) crumbs and melted margarine in a bowl. Press the mixture into the base of the prepared tin (pan).

3 Put the chopped dates, lemon juice, lemon rind and water into a saucepan and bring to the boil.

4 Simmer for 5 minutes until the dates are soft, then mash them roughly.

5 Place the mixture in a blender or food processor with the tofu (bean curd), apple juice, mashed banana and vanilla flavouring (extract) and process until the mixture is a thick, smooth purée.

6 Pour the tofu (bean curd) purée into the prepared biscuit (cracker) crumb base.

7 Bake in a preheated oven, 180°C/350°F/Gas Mark 4, for 30-40 minutes until lightly golden. Leave to cool in the tin (pan), then chill before serving.

8 Place the chopped mango in a blender and process until smooth. Serve it as a sauce with the chilled cheesecake.

Eggless Sponge

This is a healthy variation of the classic Victoria sponge cake (sponge layer cake) and is suitable for vegans.

NUTRITIONAL INFORMATION

Calories 273	Sugars 27g	
Protein 3g	Fat 9g	
Carbohydrate ...49g	Saturates 1g	

🥧 1¼ HOURS   🕐 30 MINS

1 x 8" CAKE

INGREDIENTS

225 g/8 oz/1¾ cups self-raising wholemeal (whole wheat) flour

2 tsp baking powder

175 g/6 oz/¾ cup caster (superfine) sugar

6 tbsp sunflower oil

250 ml/9 fl oz/1 cup water

1 tsp vanilla flavouring (extract)

4 tbsp strawberry or raspberry reduced-sugar spread

caster (superfine) sugar, for dusting

1 Grease two 20 cm/8 inch sandwich cake tins (layer pans) and line them with baking parchment.

2 Sieve (strain) the self-raising flour and baking powder into a large mixing bowl, stirring in any bran remaining in the sieve. Stir in the caster (superfine) sugar.

3 Pour in the sunflower oil, water and vanilla flavouring (extract). Mix well with a wooden spoon for about 1 minute until the mixture is smooth, then divide between the prepared tins (pans).

4 Bake in a preheated oven, 180°C/ 350°F/Gas Mark 4, for about 25-30 minutes until the centre springs back when lightly touched.

5 Leave the sponges to cool in the tins (pans) before turning out and transferring to a wire rack.

6 To serve, remove the baking parchment and place one of the sponges on to a serving plate. Spread with the jam and place the other sponge on top.

7 Dust the eggless sponge cake with a little caster (superfine) sugar before serving.

Banana & Lime Cake

A substantial cake that is ideal served for tea. The mashed bananas help to keep the cake moist, and the lime icing gives it extra zing and zest.

NUTRITIONAL INFORMATION

Calories . . . . . . .235 Sugars 31g
Protein . . . . .5g Fat 1g
Carbohydrate . . .55g Saturates 0.3g

 35 MINS   🕐 45 MINS

SERVES 10

I N G R E D I E N T S

300 g/10½ oz plain (all-purpose) flour

1 tsp salt

1½ tsp baking powder

175 g/6 oz light muscovado sugar

1 tsp lime rind, grated

1 medium egg, beaten

1 medium banana, mashed with 1 tbsp
    lime juice

150 ml/5 fl oz/⅔ cup low-fat natural
    fromage frais (unsweetened yogurt)

115 g/4 oz sultanas

banana chips, to decorate

lime rind, finely grated, to decorate

T O P P I N G

115 g/4 oz icing (confectioners') sugar

1–2 tsp lime juice

½ tsp lime rind, finely grated

1 Preheat the oven to 180°C/350°F/Gas Mark 4. Grease and line a deep 18 cm/7 inch round cake tin with baking parchment.

2 Sift the flour, salt and baking powder into a mixing bowl and stir in the sugar and lime rind.

3 Make a well in the centre of the dry ingredients and add the egg, banana, fromage frais (yogurt) and sultanas. Mix well until thoroughly incorporated.

4 Spoon the mixture into the tin and smooth the surface. Bake for 40–45 minutes until firm to the touch or until a skewer inserted in the centre comes out clean. Leave to cool for 10 minutes, then turn out on to a wire rack.

5 To make the topping, sift the icing (confectioners') sugar into a small bowl and mix with the lime juice to form a soft, but not too runny, icing. Stir in the grated lime rind. Drizzle the icing over the cake, letting it run down the sides.

6 Decorate the cake with banana chips and lime rind. Let the cake stand for 15 minutes so that the icing sets.

VARIATION

For a delicious alternative, replace the lime rind and juice with orange and the sultanas with chopped apricots.

Crispy-Topped Fruit Bake

The sugar cubes give a lovely crunchy taste to this easy-to-make pudding.

NUTRITIONAL INFORMATION

Calories 227   Sugars 30g
Protein . . . . .5g   Fat 1g
Carbohydrate . . .53g   Saturates 0.2g

15 MINS   1 HOUR

SERVES 10

INGREDIENTS

350 g/12 oz cooking apples

3 tbsp lemon juice

300 g/10½ oz self-raising wholemeal (whole wheat) flour

½ tsp baking powder

1 tsp ground cinnamon, plus extra for dusting

175 g/6 oz prepared blackberries, thawed if frozen, plus extra to decorate

175 g/6 oz light muscovado sugar

1 medium egg, beaten

200 ml/7 fl oz/¾ cup low-fat natural fromage frais (unsweetened yogurt)

60 g/2 oz white or brown sugar cubes, lightly crushed

sliced eating (dessert) apple, to decorate

1 Preheat the oven to 190°C/375°F/Gas Mark 5. Grease and line a 900 g/2 lb loaf tin (pan). Core, peel and finely dice the apples. Place them in a saucepan with the lemon juice, bring to the boil, cover and simmer for 10 minutes until soft and pulpy. Beat well and set aside to cool.

2 Sift the flour, baking powder and 1 tsp cinnamon into a bowl, adding any husks that remain in the sieve. Stir in 115 g/4 oz blackberries and the sugar.

3 Make a well in the centre of the ingredients and add the egg, fromage frais (unsweetened yogurt) and cooled apple purée. Mix well to incorporate thoroughly. Spoon the mixture into the prepared loaf tin (pan) and smooth over the top.

4 Sprinkle with the remaining blackberries, pressing them down into the cake mixture, and top with the crushed sugar lumps. Bake for 40–45 minutes. Leave to cool in the tin (pan).

5 Remove the cake from the tin (pan) and peel away the lining paper. Serve dusted with cinnamon and decorated with extra blackberries and apple slices.

VARIATION

Try replacing the blackberries with blueberries. Use the canned or frozen variety if fresh blueberries are unavailable.

Rich Chocolate Loaf

Another rich chocolate dessert, this loaf is very simple to make and can be served as a tea-time treat as well.

NUTRITIONAL INFORMATION

Calories 180	Sugars 16g
Protein 3g	Fat 11g
Carbohydrate ...18g	Saturates 5g

1¼ HOURS 5 MINS

MAKES 16 SLICES

I N G R E D I E N T S

150 g/5½ oz dark chocolate

75 g/2¾ oz/6 tbsp butter, unsalted

210 g/7¼ oz tin of condensed milk

2 tsp cinnamon

75 g/2¾ oz almonds

75 g/2¾ oz amaretti biscuits (cookies), broken

50 g/1¾ oz dried no-need-to-soak apricots, roughly chopped

1 Line a 675 g/1½ lb loaf tin (pan) with a sheet of kitchen foil.

2 Using a sharp knife, roughly chop the almonds.

3 Place the chocolate, butter, milk and cinnamon in a heavy-based saucepan.

COOK'S TIP

To melt chocolate, first break it into manageable pieces. The smaller the pieces, the quicker it will melt.

4 Heat the chocolate mixture over a low heat for 3–4 minutes, stirring with a wooden spoon, or until the chocolate has melted. Beat the mixture well.

5 Stir the almonds, biscuits and apricots into the chocolate mixture, stirring with a wooden spoon, until well mixed.

6 Pour the mixture into the prepared tin (pan) and leave to chill in the refrigerator for about 1 hour or until set.

7 Cut the rich chocolate loaf into slices to serve.

Chocolate Biscotti

These dry biscuits (cookies) are delicious served with black coffee after your evening meal.

NUTRITIONAL INFORMATION

Calories . . . . .113 Sugars 9g
Protein . . . . .2g Fat 5g
Carbohydrate . . .15g Saturates 1g

 20 MINS   40 MINS

MAKES 16

INGREDIENTS

1 egg

100 g/3½ oz/⅓ cup caster (superfine) sugar

1 tsp vanilla essence (extract)

125 g/4½ oz/1 cup plain (all-purpose) flour

½ tsp baking powder

1 tsp ground cinnamon

50 g/1¾ oz dark chocolate, chopped roughly

50 g/1¾ oz toasted flaked (slivered) almonds

50 g/1¾ oz pine kernels (nuts)

1 Lightly grease a large baking tray (cookie sheet).

2 Whisk the egg, sugar and vanilla essence (extract) in a mixing bowl with an electric mixer until it is thick and pale – ribbons of mixture should trail from the whisk as you lift it.

3 Sieve (strain) the flour, baking powder and cinnamon into a separate bowl, then sieve (strain) into the egg mixture and fold in gently. Stir in the chocolate, almonds and pine kernels (nuts).

4 Turn on to a lightly floured surface and shape into a flat log, 23 cm/ 9 inches long and 1.5 cm/¾ inch wide. Transfer to the baking tray (cookie sheet).

5 Bake in a preheated oven, at 180°C/ 350°F/Gas Mark 4, for 20-25 minutes or until golden. Remove from the oven and leave to cool for 5 minutes or until firm.

6 Transfer the log to a cutting board. Using a serrated bread knife, cut the log on the diagonal into slices about 1 cm/ ½ inch thick and arrange them on the baking tray (cookie sheet). Cook for 10-15 minutes, turning halfway through the cooking time.

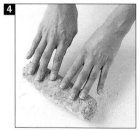

7 Leave to cool for about 5 minutes, then transfer to a wire rack to cool completely.

Florentine Twists

These famous and delicious Florentine biscuits (cookies) are twisted into curls or cones and then just the ends are dipped in chocolate.

NUTRITIONAL INFORMATION

Calories	28	Sugars	.......15g
Protein	.........1g	Fat	...........7g
Carbohydrate	...15g	Saturates	.......4g

🍴 20 MINS   🕐 20 MINS

MAKES 20

I N G R E D I E N T S

90 g/3 oz/⅓ cup butter

125 g/4½ oz/½ cup caster (superfine) sugar

60 g/2 oz/½ cup blanched or flaked (slivered) almonds, chopped roughly

25 g/1 oz/3 tbsp raisins, chopped

45 g/1½ oz/¼ cup chopped mixed peel

45 g/1½ oz/scant ¼ cup glacé (candied) cherries, chopped

25 g/1 oz/3 tbsp dried apricots, chopped finely

finely grated rind of ½ lemon or ½ small orange

about 125 g/4½ oz/4 squares dark or white chocolate

1 Line 2–3 baking trays (cookie sheets) with non-stick baking parchment; then grease 4–6 cream horn tins (moulds) or a fairly thin rolling pin, or wooden spoon handles.

2 Melt the butter and sugar together gently in a saucepan and then bring to the boil for 1 minute. Remove the pan from the heat and stir in all the remaining ingredients, except for the chocolate. Leave to cool.

3 Put heaped teaspoonfuls of the mixture on to the baking sheets, keeping them well apart, only 3–4 per sheet, and flatten slightly.

4 Bake in a preheated oven, at 180°C/ 350°F/Gas Mark 4, for 10–12 minutes, or until golden. Leave to cool until they begin to firm up. As they cool, press the edges back to form a neat shape. Remove each one with a palette knife (spatula) and wrap quickly around a cream horn tin (mould), or lay over the rolling pin or spoon handles. If they become too firm to bend, return to the oven briefly to soften.

5 Leave until cold and crisp and then slip carefully off the horn tins (moulds) or remove from the rolling pin or spoons.

6 Melt the chocolate in a heatproof bowl over a saucepan of hot water, or in a microwave oven set on Full Power for about 45 seconds, and stir until smooth. Either dip the end of each Florentine twist into the chocolate or, using a pastry brush, paint chocolate to come about halfway up the twist. As the chocolate sets, it can be marked into wavy lines with a fork. Leave to set.

Chocolate Brownies

You really can have a low-fat chocolate treat. These moist bars contain a dried fruit purée, which enables you to bake without adding any fat.

NUTRITIONAL INFORMATION

Calories 271   Sugars 45g
Protein . . . . .5g   Fat 4g
Carbohydrate . . .57g   Saturates 2g

🥧 30 MINS   🕐 40 MINS

MAKES 12

INGREDIENTS

60 g/2 oz unsweetened pitted dates, chopped

60 g/2 oz no-need-to-soak dried prunes, chopped

6 tbsp unsweetened apple juice

4 medium eggs, beaten

300 g/10½ oz dark muscovado sugar

1 tsp vanilla essence (extract)

4 tbsp low-fat drinking chocolate powder, plus extra for dusting

2 tbsp cocoa powder

175 g/6 oz plain (all-purpose) flour

60 g/2 oz dark chocolate chips

ICING

125 g/4½ oz icing (confectioners') sugar

1–2 tsp water

1 tsp vanilla essence (extract)

COOK'S TIP

Make double the amount, cut one of the cakes into bars and open freeze, then store in plastic bags. Take out pieces of cake as and when you need them - they'll take no time at all to defrost.

1 Preheat the oven to 180°C/350°F/Gas Mark 4. Grease and line a 18 x 28 cm/7 x 11 inch cake tin with baking parchment. Place the dates and prunes in a small saucepan and add the apple juice. Bring to the boil, cover and simmer for 10 minutes until soft. Beat to form a smooth paste, then set aside to cool.

2 Place the cooled fruit in a mixing bowl and stir in the eggs, sugar and vanilla essence. Sift in 4 tbsp drinking chocolate, the cocoa and the flour, and fold in along with the chocolate chips until well incorporated.

3 Spoon the mixture into the prepared tin and smooth over the top. Bake for 25–30 minutes until firm to the touch or until a skewer inserted into the centre comes out clean. Cut into 12 bars and leave to cool in the tin for 10 minutes. Transfer to a wire rack to cool completely.

4 To make the icing (frosting), sift the sugar into a bowl and mix with sufficient water and the vanilla essence (extract) to form a soft, but not too runny, icing (frosting).

5 Drizzle the icing (frosting) over the chocolate brownies and allow to set. Dust with the extra chocolate powder before serving.

Rosemary Biscuits (Cookies)

Do not be put off by the idea of herbs being used in these crisp biscuits (cookies) – try them and you will be pleasantly surprised.

NUTRITIONAL INFORMATION

Calories ....50 Sugars 2g
Protein ....1g Fat 2g
Carbohydrate ....8g Saturates 1g

45 MINS   15 MINS

MAKES 25

INGREDIENTS

50 g/1¾ oz/10 tsp butter, softened

4 tbsp caster (superfine) sugar

grated rind of 1 lemon

4 tbsp lemon juice

1 egg, separated

2 tsp finely chopped fresh rosemary

200 g/7 oz/1¾ cups plain (all-purpose)
    flour, sieved (strained)

caster (superfine) sugar, for sprinkling
    (optional)

1 Lightly grease 2 baking trays (cookie sheets).

2 In a large mixing bowl, cream together the butter and sugar until pale and fluffy.

3 Add the lemon rind and juice, then the egg yolk and beat until they are thoroughly combined. Stir in the chopped fresh rosemary.

4 Add the sieved (strained) flour, mixing well until a soft dough is formed. Wrap and leave to chill for 30 minutes.

5 On a lightly floured surface, roll out the dough thinly and then stamp out 25 circles with a 6 cm/2½ inch biscuit (cookie) cutter. Arrange the dough circles on the prepared baking trays (cookie sheets).

6 In a bowl, lightly whisk the egg white. Gently brush the egg white over the surface of each biscuit (cookie), then sprinkle with a little caster (superfine) sugar, if liked.

7 Bake in a preheated oven, at 180°C/ 350°F/Gas Mark 4, for about 15 minutes.

8 Transfer the biscuits (cookies) to a wire rack and leave to cool before serving.

COOK'S TIP

Store the biscuits (cookies) in an airtight container for up to 1 week.

Almond Slices

A mouth-watering dessert that is sure to impress your guests, especially if it is served with whipped cream.

NUTRITIONAL INFORMATION

Calories	416	Sugars	........37g
Protein	........11g	Fat	..........26g
Carbohydrate	...38g	Saturates	......12g

 5 MINS   🕐 5 MINS

SERVES 8

INGREDIENTS

3 eggs

75 g/2¾ oz/½ cup ground almonds

200 g/7 oz/1½ cups milk powder

200 g/7 oz/1 cup sugar

½ tsp saffron strands

100 g/3½ oz/½ cup unsalted butter

25 g/1 oz/1 tbsp flaked (slivered) almonds

1 Beat the eggs together in a bowl and set aside.

2 Place the ground almonds, milk powder, sugar and saffron in a large mixing bowl and stir to mix well.

3 Melt the butter in a small saucepan. Pour the melted butter over the dry ingredients and mix well until thoroughly combined.

4 Add the reserved beaten eggs to the mixture and stir to blend well.

5 Spread the mixture in a shallow 15–20 cm/7–9 inch ovenproof dish and bake in a preheated oven, 160°C/325°F/Gas Mark 3, for 45 minutes. Test whether the cake is cooked through by piercing with the tip of a sharp knife or a skewer – it will come out clean if it is cooked thoroughly.

6 Cut the almond cake into slices. Decorate the almond slices with flaked (slivered) almonds and transfer to serving plates. Serve hot or cold.

COOK'S TIP

These almond slices are best eaten hot, but they may also be served cold. They can be made a day or even a week in advance and re-heated. They also freeze beautifully.

Christmas Shortbread

Make this wonderful shortbread and then give it the Christmas touch by cutting it into shapes with seasonal biscuit (cookie) cutters.

NUTRITIONAL INFORMATION

Calories ....162 Sugars 10g
Protein ....1g Fat 9g
Carbohydrate ...21g Saturates 6g

🍰 45 MINS   🕐 15 MINS

MAKES 24

I N G R E D I E N T S

125 g/4½ oz/½ cup caster
    (superfine) sugar

225 g/8 oz/1 cup butter

350 g/12 oz/3 cups plain (all-purpose)
    flour, sifted

pinch of salt

T O   D E C O R A T E

60 g/2 oz/½ cup icing
    (confectioners') sugar

silver balls

glacé (candied) cherries

angelica

1 Beat the sugar and butter together in a large bowl until combined (thorough creaming is not necessary).

2 Sift in the flour and salt and work together to form a stiff dough. Turn out on to a lightly floured surface. Knead lightly for a few moments until smooth, but avoid overhandling. Chill in the refrigerator for 10–15 minutes.

3 Roll out the dough on a lightly floured work surface and cut into shapes with small Christmas cutters, such as bells, stars and angels. Place on greased baking trays (cookie sheets).

4 Bake the biscuits (cookies) in a preheated oven, 180°C/350°F/Gas Mark 4 for 10–15 minutes, until pale golden brown. Leave on the baking trays (cookie sheets) for 10 minutes, then transfer to wire racks to cool completely.

5 Mix the icing (confectioners') sugar with a little water to make a glacé icing (frosting), and use to ice (frost) the biscuits (cookies). Decorate with silver balls, tiny pieces of glacé (candied) cherries and angelica. Store in an airtight container or wrap the biscuits (cookies) individually in cellophane, tie with coloured ribbon or string and then hang them on the Christmas tree as edible decorations.

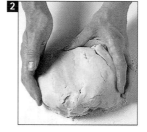  

Potato Muffins

These light-textured muffins rise like little soufflés in the oven and are best eaten warm. The dried fruits can be varied according to taste.

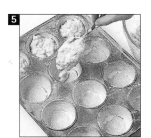

NUTRITIONAL INFORMATION

Calories	98	Sugars	........11g
Protein	.........3g	Fat	..........2g
Carbohydrate	...18g	Saturates	.....0.5g

  20 MINS 🕐 35 MINS

MAKES 12

I N G R E D I E N T S

175 g/6 oz floury (mealy) potatoes, diced

75 g/2¾ oz/¾ cup self-raising (self-rising) flour

2 tbsp soft light brown sugar

1 tsp baking powder

125 g/4½ oz/¾ cup raisins

4 eggs, separated

1 Lightly grease and flour 12 muffin tins (pans).

2 Cook the diced potatoes in a saucepan of boiling water for 10 minutes, or until tender. Drain well and mash until completely smooth.

3 Transfer the mashed potatoes to a mixing bowl and add the flour, sugar, baking powder, raisins and egg yolks. Stir well to mix thoroughly.

4 In a clean bowl, whisk the egg whites until standing in peaks. Using a metal spoon, gently fold them into the potato mixture until fully incorporated.

5 Divide the mixture between the prepared tins (pans).

6 Cook in a preheated oven, 200°C/ 400°F/Gas Mark 6, for 10 minutes. Reduce the oven temperature to 160°C/ 325°F/Gas Mark 3 and cook the muffins for a further 7-10 minutes, or until risen.

7 Remove the muffins from the tins (pans) and serve warm.

COOK'S TIP

Instead of spreading the muffins with plain butter, serve them with cinnamon butter made by blending 60 g/2 oz/½ cup butter with a large pinch of ground cinnamon.

Almond & Pistachio Dessert

Rich and mouth-watering, this dessert can be prepared well in advance of the meal. It is best served cold.

NUTRITIONAL INFORMATION

Calories 565	Sugars 37g	
Protein 8g	Fat 43g	
Carbohydrate ...38g	Saturates 16g	

1¼ HOURS   15 MINS

SERVES 6

INGREDIENTS

75 g/2¾ oz/6 tbsp unsalted (sweet) butter

200 g/7 oz/1¾ cups ground almonds

200 g/7 oz/1 cup sugar

150 ml/¼ pint/⅔ cup single (light) cream

8 almonds, chopped

10 pistachio nuts, chopped

1 Place the butter in a medium-size saucepan, preferably non-stick. Melt the butter, stirring well.

2 Add the ground almonds, cream and sugar to the melted butter in the pan, stirring to combine. Reduce the heat and stir constantly for 10-12 minutes, scraping the base of the pan.

3 Increase the heat until the mixture turns a little darker in colour.

COOK'S TIP

This almond dessert can be made in advance and stored in an airtight container in the refrigerator for several days. You could use a variety of shaped pastry cutters, to cut the dessert into different shapes, rather than diamonds, if you prefer.

4 Transfer the almond mixture to a shallow serving dish and smooth the top with the back of a spoon.

5 Decorate the top of the dessert with the chopped almonds and pistachios.

6 Leave the dessert to set for about 1 hour, then cut into diamond shapes and serve cold.

Almond Cheesecakes

These creamy cheese desserts are so delicious that it's hard to believe that they are low in fat.

NUTRITIONAL INFORMATION

Calories 361	Sugars 29g
Protein 16g	Fat 15g
Carbohydrate . . .43g	Saturates 4g

🖐 🖐

🍰 1¼ HOURS   🕐 10 MINS

SERVES 4

I N G R E D I E N T S

12 Amaretti di Saronno biscuits

1 medium egg white, lightly beaten

225 g/8 oz skimmed-milk soft cheese

½ tsp almond essence (extract)

½ tsp finely grated lime rind

25 g/1 oz ground almonds

25 g/1 oz caster (superfine) sugar

60 g/2 oz sultanas (golden raisins)

2 tsp powdered gelatine

2 tbsp boiling water

2 tbsp lime juice

T O   D E C O R A T E

25 g/1 oz flaked (slivered) toasted almonds

strips of lime rind

1 Preheat the oven to 180°C/350°F/Gas Mark 4. Place the biscuits in a clean plastic bag, seal the bag and using a rolling pin, crush them into small pieces.

2 Place the crumbs in a bowl and bind together with the egg white.

3 Arrange 4 non-stick pastry rings or poached egg rings, 9 cm/3½ inches across, on a baking tray (cookie sheet) lined with baking parchment. Divide the biscuit mixture into 4 equal portions and spoon it into the rings, pressing down well. Bake for 10 minutes until crisp and leave to cool in the rings.

4 Beat together the soft cheese, almond essence (extract), lime rind, ground almonds, sugar and sultanas until well mixed.

5 Dissolve the gelatine in the boiling water and stir in the lime juice. Fold into the cheese mixture and spoon over the biscuit bases. Smooth over the tops and chill for 1 hour or until set.

6 Loosen the cheesecakes from the tins using a small palette knife or spatula and transfer to serving plates. Decorate with flaked (slivered) toasted almonds and strips of lime rind, and serve.

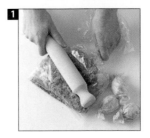

Chocolate Fudge Pudding

This pudding has a hidden surprise when cooked, as it separates to give a rich chocolate sauce at the bottom of the dish.

NUTRITIONAL INFORMATION

Calories	397	Sugars 27g
Protein	........10g	Fat 25g
Carbohydrate	...36g	Saturates 5g

🧊 10 MINS   🕐 40 MINS

SERVES 4

INGREDIENTS

50 g/1¾ oz/4 tbsp margarine, plus extra
 for greasing

75 g/2¾ oz/6 tbsp light brown sugar

2 eggs, beaten

350 ml/12 fl oz/1¼ cups milk

50 g/1¾ oz/½ cup chopped walnuts

40 g/1½ oz/¼ cup plain (all-purpose) flour

2 tbsp cocoa powder (unsweetened cocoa

icing (confectioners') sugar and cocoa

 powder (unsweetened cocoa), to dust

1 Lightly grease a 1 litre/1¾ pint/4 cup ovenproof dish.

2 Cream together the margarine and sugar in a large mixing bowl until fluffy. Beat in the eggs.

VARIATION

Add 1–2 tbsp brandy
or rum to the mixture for a
slightly alcoholic pudding, or
1–2 tbsp orange juice for a
child-friendly version.

3 Gradually stir in the milk and add the walnuts, stirring to mix.

4 Sift the flour and cocoa powder (unsweetened cocoa) into the mixture and fold in gently, with a metal spoon, until well mixed.

5 Spoon the mixture into the dish and cook in a preheated oven, 180°C/350°F/Gas Mark 4, for 35–40 minutes, or until the sponge is cooked.

6 Dust with sugar and cocoa powder (unsweetened cocoa) and serve.

Italian Bread Pudding

This deliciously rich pudding is cooked with cream and apples and is delicately flavoured with orange.

NUTRITIONAL INFORMATION

Calories	387	Sugars	........31g
Protein	.........8g	Fat	..........20g
Carbohydrate	...45g	Saturates	......12g

45 MINS 25 MINS

SERVES 4

I N G R E D I E N T S

15 g/½ oz/1 tbsp butter

2 small eating apples, peeled, cored and
  sliced into rings

75 g/2¾ oz granulated sugar

2 tbsp white wine

100 g/3½ oz bread, sliced with crusts
  removed (slightly stale French baguette
  is ideal)

300 ml/½ pint/1¼ cups single (light) cream

2 eggs, beaten

pared rind of 1 orange, cut into matchsticks

1 Lightly grease a 1.2 litre/2 pint deep ovenproof dish with the butter.

2 Arrange the apple rings in the base of the dish. Sprinkle half of the sugar over the apples.

3 Pour the wine over the apples. Add the bread slices, pushing them down with your hands to flatten them slightly.

4 Mix the cream with the eggs, the remaining sugar and the orange rind and pour the mixture over the bread. Leave to soak for 30 minutes.

5 Bake the pudding in a preheated oven, at 180°C/350°F/Gas Mark 4, for 25 minutes until golden and set. Serve warm.

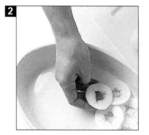  

VARIATION

For a variation, try adding dried fruit, such as apricots, cherries or dates, to the pudding, if you prefer.

Banana Pastries

These pastries require a little time to prepare, but are well worth the effort. A sweet banana filling is wrapped in dough and baked.

NUTRITIONAL INFORMATION

Calories	745	Sugars	........24g
Protein	........13g	Fat	..........30g
Carbohydrate	...112g	Saturates	......15g

  45 MINS   25 MINS

SERVES 4

I N G R E D I E N T S

DOUGH

450 g/1 lb/4 cups plain (all-purpose) flour

60 g/2 oz/4 tbsp lard (shortening)

60 g/2 oz/4 tbsp unsalted butter

125 ml/4 fl oz/½ cup water

FILLING

2 large bananas

75 g/2¾ oz/⅓ cup finely chopped
   no-need-to-soak dried apricots

pinch of nutmeg

dash of orange juice

1 egg yolk, beaten

icing (confectioners') sugar, for dusting

cream or ice cream, to serve

1 To make the dough, sift the flour into a large mixing bowl. Add the lard (shortening) and butter and rub into the flour with the fingertips until the mixture resembles breadcrumbs. Gradually blend in the water to make a soft dough. Wrap in cling film (plastic wrap) and chill in the refrigerator for 30 minutes.

2 Mash the bananas in a bowl with a fork and stir in the apricots, nutmeg and orange juice, mixing well.

3 Roll the dough out on a lightly floured surface and cut out 16 x 10-cm/4-inch rounds.

4 Spoon a little of the banana filling on to one half of each round and fold the dough over the filling to make semi-circles. Pinch the edges together and seal by pressing with the prongs of a fork.

5 Arrange the pastries on a non-stick baking tray (cookie sheet) and brush them with the beaten egg yolk. Cut a small slit in each pastry and cook in a preheated oven, 180°C/350°F/Gas 4, for about 25 minutes, or until golden brown.

6 Dust the banana pastries with icing (confectioners') sugar and serve with cream or ice cream.

VARIATION

Use a fruit filling of your choice, such as apple or plum, as an alternative.

Honeyed Rice Puddings

These small rice puddings are quite sweet, but have a wonderful flavour because of the combination of ginger, honey and cinnamon.

NUTRITIONAL INFORMATION

Calories	199	Sugars	........15g
Protein	.........3g	Fat	...........1g
Carbohydrate	...46g	Saturates	.......0g

10 MINS   50 MINS

SERVES 4

I N G R E D I E N T S

300 g/10½ oz/1½ cups pudding rice

2 tbsp clear honey, plus extra
  for drizzling

large pinch of ground cinnamon

15 no-need-to-soak dried apricots,
  chopped

3 pieces stem (preserved) ginger, drained
  and chopped

8 whole no-need-to-soak dried apricots,
  to decorate

1 Put the rice in a saucepan and just cover with cold water. Bring to the boil, reduce the heat, cover and cook for about 15 minutes, or until the water has been absorbed. Stir the honey and cinnamon into the rice.

2 Grease 4 x 150 ml/¼ pint/⅔ cup ramekin dishes.

3 Blend the chopped dried apricots and ginger in a food processor to make a smooth paste.

4 Divide the paste into 4 equal portions and shape each into a flat round to fit into the base of the ramekin dishes.

5 Divide half of the rice between the ramekin dishes and place the apricot paste on top.

6 Cover the apricot paste with the remaining rice. Cover the ramekins with greaseproof (wax) paper and foil and steam for 30 minutes, or until set.

7 Remove the ramekins from the steamer and let stand for 5 minutes.

8 Turn the puddings out on to warm serving plates and drizzle with honey. Decorate with dried apricots and serve.

COOK'S TIP

The puddings may be left to chill in their ramekin dishes in the refrigerator, then turned out and served with ice cream or cream.

Fruity Queen of Puddings

A scrumptious version of a classic British pudding, made here with fresh bananas and apricot jam (jelly).

NUTRITIONAL INFORMATION

Calories 406   Sugars 60g
Protein . . . . .13g   Fat 7g
Carbohydrate . . .77g   Saturates 3g

30 MINS   1 HOUR

SERVES 4

INGREDIENTS

125 g/4½ oz/2 cups fresh white breadcrumbs

600 ml/1 pint/2½ cups milk

3 eggs

½ tsp vanilla essence (extract)

60 g/2 oz/¼ cup caster (superfine) sugar

2 bananas

1 tbsp lemon juice

3 tbsp apricot jam (jelly)

1 Sprinkle the breadcrumbs into a 1 litre/1¾ pint/4 cup ovenproof dish. Heat the milk until lukewarm, then pour it over the breadcrumbs.

2 Separate 2 of the eggs and beat the yolks with the remaining whole egg. Add to the dish with the vanilla essence (extract) and half the sugar, stirring well to mix. Allow to stand for 10 minutes.

COOK'S TIP

The meringue will have a soft, marshmallow-like texture, unlike a hard meringue which is cooked slowly for 2–3 hours, until dry. Always use a grease-free bowl and whisk for beating egg-whites, otherwise they will not whip properly.

3 Bake in a preheated oven, 180°C/ 350°F/Gas Mark 4, for 40, minutes until set. Remove from the oven.

4 Slice the bananas and sprinkle with the lemon juice. Spoon the apricot jam (jelly) on to the pudding and spread out to cover the surface. Arrange the bananas on top of the apricot jam (jelly).

5 Whisk the egg whites until stiff, then add the remaining sugar. Continue whisking until the meringue is very stiff and glossy.

6 Pile the meringue on top of the pudding, return to the oven and cook for a further 10–15 minutes, until set and golden brown. Serve immediately.

Steamed Coffee Sponge

This sponge pudding is very light and is quite delicious served with a sweet chocolate sauce.

NUTRITIONAL INFORMATION

Calories	300	Sugars	.......21g
Protein	.........8g	Fat	..........13g
Carbohydrate	...40g	Saturates	.......4g

  10 MINS

1¼ HOURS

SERVES 4

I N G R E D I E N T S

25 g/1 oz/2 tbsp margarine

2 tbsp soft brown sugar

2 eggs

50 g/1¾ oz/⅓ cup plain (all-purpose) flour

¾ tsp baking powder

6 tbsp milk

1 tsp coffee flavouring (extract)

S A U C E

300 ml/½ pint/1¼ cups milk

1 tbsp soft brown sugar

1 tsp cocoa powder
  (unsweetened) cocoa

2 tbsp cornflour (cornstarch)

COOK'S TIP

The pudding is covered with pleated paper and foil to allow it to rise. The foil will react with the steam and must therefore not be placed directly against the pudding.

1 Lightly grease a 600 ml/1 pint/2½ cup pudding basin (heatproof bowl). Cream the margarine and sugar until light and fluffy and beat in the eggs.

2 Gradually stir in the flour and baking powder and then the milk and coffee flavouring (extract) to make a smooth batter.

3 Spoon the mixture into the prepared pudding basin (heatproof bowl) and cover with a pleated piece of baking parchment and then a pleated piece of foil, securing around the bowl with string. Place in a steamer or large pan and half fill with boiling water. Cover and steam for 1–1¼ hours, or until cooked through.

4 To make the sauce, put the milk, soft brown sugar and cocoa powder (unsweetened cocoa) in a pan and heat , stirring constantly, until the sugar dissolves. Blend the cornflour (cornstarch) with 4 tablespoons of cold water to make a smooth paste and stir into the pan. Bring to the boil, stirring constantly until thickened. Cook over a gentle heat for 1 minute.

5 Turn the pudding out on to a warmed serving plate and spoon the sauce over the top. Serve immediately.

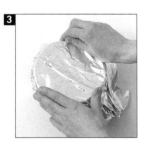

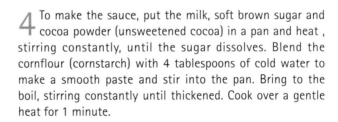

Quick Syrup Sponge

You won't believe your eyes when you see just how quickly this light-as-air sponge pudding cooks in the microwave oven!

NUTRITIONAL INFORMATION

Calories 650   Sugars 60g
Protein . . . . .10g   Fat 31g
Carbohydrate . . .89g   Saturates 7g

🍲 15 MINS   🕐 5 MINS

SERVES 4

INGREDIENTS

125 g/4½ oz/½ cup butter or margarine

4 tbsp golden (light corn) syrup

90 g/3 oz/⅓ cup caster (superfine) sugar

2 eggs

125 g/4½ oz/1 cup self-raising
   (self-rising) flour

1 tsp baking powder

about 2 tbsp warm water

custard, to serve

1 Grease a 1.5 litre/2½ pint/1½ quart pudding basin (heatproof bowl) with a small amount of the butter or margarine. Spoon the syrup into the basin (bowl).

2 Cream the remaining butter or margarine with the sugar until light and fluffy. Gradually add the eggs, beating well between each addition.

3 Sift the flour and baking powder together, then fold into the creamed mixture using a large metal spoon. Add enough water to give a soft, dropping consistency. Spoon into the pudding basin (bowl) and level the surface.

4 Cover with microwave-safe film, leaving a small space to allow air to escape. Microwave on HIGH power for

4 minutes, then remove from the microwave and allow the pudding to stand for 5 minutes, while it continues to cook.

5 Turn the pudding out on to a serving plate. Serve with custard.

COOK'S TIP

If you don't have a microwave, this pudding can be steamed. Cover the with a piece of pleated baking parchment and a piece of pleated foil. Place in a saucepan, add boiling water and steam for 1½ hours.

Mixed Fruit Crumble

In this crumble, tropical fruits are flavoured with ginger and coconut, for something a little different and very tasty.

NUTRITIONAL INFORMATION

Calories	602	Sugars	........51g
Protein	.........6g	Fat	..........29g
Carbohydrate	...84g	Saturates	......11g

10 MINS   50 MINS

SERVES 4

INGREDIENTS

2 mangoes, sliced

1 paw paw (papaya), seeded and sliced

225 g/8 oz fresh pineapple, cubed

1½ tsp ground ginger

100 g/3½ oz/½ cup margarine

100 g/3½ oz/½ cup light brown sugar

175 g/6 oz/1½ cups plain (all-purpose) flour

50 g/1¾ oz/1 cup desiccated (shredded)
   coconut, plus extra to decorate

 Place the fruit in a pan with ½ tsp of the ginger, 30 g/1 oz/2 tbsp of the margarine and 50 g/1¾ oz/¼ cup of the sugar. Cook over a low heat for 10 minutes, until the fruit softens. Spoon the fruit into the base of a shallow ovenproof dish.

VARIATION

Use other fruits, such as plums, apples or blackberries, as a fruit base and add chopped nuts to the topping instead of the coconut.

2 Mix the flour and remaining ginger together. Rub in the remaining margarine until the mixture resembles fine breadcrumbs. Stir in the remaining sugar and the coconut and spoon over the fruit to cover completely.

3 Cook the crumble in a preheated oven, 180°C/ 350°F/Gas Mark 4, for about 40 minutes, or until the top is crisp. Decorate and serve.

Saffron-Spiced Rice Pudding

This rich pudding is cooked in milk delicately flavoured with saffron, then mixed with dried fruit, almonds and cream before baking.

NUTRITIONAL INFORMATION

Calories	....	.339
Protein	....	.9g
Carbohydrate	...	41g

Sugars	....	.28g
Fat	....	.16g
Saturates	....	.9g

 5 MINS   🕐 1 HOUR

SERVES 4

I N G R E D I E N T S

600 ml/1 pint/2½ cups creamy milk

several pinches of saffron strands, finely crushed (see Cook's Tip)

60 g/2 oz/¼ cup short grain (pudding) rice

1 cinnamon stick or piece of cassia bark

40 g/1½ oz/¼ cup sugar

25 g/1 oz/¼ cup seedless raisins or sultanas (golden raisins)

25 g/1 oz/¼ cup ready-to-eat dried apricots, chopped

1 egg, beaten

5 tbsp single (light) cream

15 g/½ oz/1 tbsp butter, diced

15 g/½ oz/2 tbsp flaked almonds

freshly grated nutmeg, for sprinkling

cream, for serving (optional)

1 Place the milk and crushed saffron in a non-stick saucepan and bring to the boil. Stir in the rice and cinnamon stick, reduce the heat and simmer very gently, uncovered, stirring frequently, for 25 minutes, until tender.

2 Remove the pan from the heat. Remove and discard the cinnamon stick from the rice mixture. Stir in the sugar, raisins or sultanas (golden raisins) and dried apricots, then beat in the egg, cream and diced butter.

3 Transfer the mixture to a greased ovenproof pie or flan dish, sprinkle with the almonds and freshly grated nutmeg to taste. Cook in a preheated oven, 180°C/350°F/Gas Mark 4, for 25–30 minutes, until mixture is set and lightly golden. Serve hot with extra cream, if wished.

COOK'S TIP

For a slightly stronger flavour, place the saffron strands on a small piece of kitchen foil and toast them lightly under a hot grill (broiler) for a few moments and then crush between your fingers and thumb.

Bread & Butter Pudding

Everyone has their own favourite recipe for this dish. This one has added marmalade and grated apples for a really rich and unique taste.

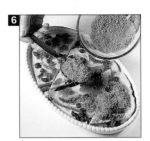

NUTRITIONAL INFORMATION

Calories 427	Sugars 63g	
Protein 9g	Fat 13g	
Carbohydrate ...74g	Saturates 7g	

   45 MINS   1 HOUR

SERVES 6

I N G R E D I E N T S

about 60 g/2 oz/¼ cup butter, softened

4–5 slices white or brown bread

4 tbsp chunky orange marmalade

grated rind of 1 lemon

90–125 g/3–4½ oz/½–¾ cup raisins or
   sultanas (golden raisins)

40 g/1½ oz/¼ cup chopped mixed
   (candied) peel

1 tsp ground cinnamon or mixed spice
   (apple spice)

1 cooking apple, peeled,
   cored and coarsely grated

90 g/3 oz/scant ½ cup light brown sugar

3 eggs

500 ml/18 fl oz/2 cups milk

2 tbsp demerara (brown crystal) sugar

1 Use the butter to grease an ovenproof dish and to spread on the slices of bread, then spread the bread with the marmalade.

2 Place a layer of bread in the base of the dish and sprinkle with the lemon rind, half the raisins or sultanas (golden raisins), half the mixed (candied) peel, half the spice, all of the apple and half the light brown sugar.

3 Add another layer of bread, cutting so it fits the dish.

4 Sprinkle over most of the remaining raisins or sultanas (golden raisins) and the remaining peel, spice and light brown sugar, sprinkling it evenly over the bread. Top with a final layer of bread, again cutting to fit the dish.

5 Lightly beat together the eggs and milk and then carefully strain the mixture over the bread in the dish. If time allows, set aside to stand for 20–30 minutes.

6 Sprinkle the top of the pudding with the demerara (brown crystal) sugar and scatter over the remaining raisins or sultanas (golden raisins) and cook in a preheated oven, 200°C/400°F/Gas Mark 6, for 50–60 minutes, until risen and golden brown. Serve immediately or allow to cool and then serve cold.

Spiced Steamed Pudding

Steamed puddings are irresistible on a winter's day, but the texture of this pudding is so light it can be served throughout the year.

NUTRITIONAL INFORMATION

Calories	488	Sugars	.....56g
Protein	.....5g	Fat	.....19g
Carbohydrate	...78g	Saturates	.....4g

15 MINS   1½ HOURS

SERVES 6

I N G R E D I E N T S

2 tbsp golden (light corn) syrup, plus extra
   to serve

125 g/4½ oz/½ cup butter or margarine

125 g/4½ oz/generous ½ cup caster
   (superfine) or light brown sugar

2 eggs

175 g/6 oz/1⅓ cups self-raising flour

¾ tsp ground cinnamon or mixed spice
   (apple spice)

grated rind of 1 orange

1 tbsp orange juice

90 g/3 oz/½ cup sultanas (golden raisins)

40 g/1½ oz/5 tbsp stem (preserved) ginger,
   finely chopped

1 eating apple, peeled, cored and
   coarsely grated

1 Thoroughly grease a 850 ml/ 1½ pint/3¾ cup pudding basin (heatproof bowl). Put the golden (light corn) syrup into the basin (bowl).

2 Cream the butter or margarine and sugar together until very light and fluffy and pale in colour. Beat in the eggs, one at a time, following each with a spoonful of the flour.

3 Sift the remaining flour with the cinnamon or mixed spice (apple spice) and fold into the mixture, followed by the orange rind and juice. Fold in the sultanas (golden raisins), then the ginger and apple.

4 Turn the mixture into the basin (bowl) and level the top. Cover with a piece of pleated greased baking parchment, tucking the edges under the rim of the basin (bowl).

5 Cover with a sheet of pleated foil. Tie securely in place with string, with a piece of string tied over the top of the basin (bowl) for a handle to make it easy to lift out of the saucepan.

6 Put the basin (bowl) into a saucepan half-filled with boiling water, cover and steam for 1½ hours, adding more boiling water to the pan as necessary during cooking.

7 To serve the pudding, remove the foil and baking parchment, turn the pudding on to a warmed serving plate and serve immediately.

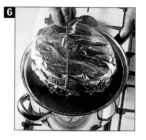

Fruity Pancake Bundles

This unusual pancake is filled with a sweet cream flavoured with ginger, nuts and apricots and served with a raspberry and orange sauce.

NUTRITIONAL INFORMATION

Calories	.610	Sugars	.60g
Protein	.19g	Fat	.20g
Carbohydrate	.94g	Saturates	.5g

15 MINS   35 MINS

SERVES 2

INGREDIENTS

BATTER

60 g/2 oz/½ cup plain (all-purpose) flour

pinch of salt

¼ tsp ground cinnamon

1 egg

135 ml/4½ fl oz/generous ½ cup milk

white vegetable fat, for frying

FILLING

1½ tsp plain (all-purpose) flour, sifted

1½ tsp cornflour (cornstarch)

1 tbsp caster (superfine) sugar

1 egg

150 ml/¼ pint/⅔ cup milk

25 g/1 oz/¼ cup chopped nuts

40 g/1½ oz/¼ cup ready-to-eat dried
   apricots, chopped

1 piece stem (preserved) or crystallized
   (candied) ginger, finely chopped

SAUCE

3 tbsp raspberry preserve

4½ tsp orange juice

finely grated rind of ¼ orange

1 To make the batter, sift the flour, salt and cinnamon into a bowl and make a well in the centre. Add the egg and beat in the flour and milk gradually until smooth.

2 Melt a little fat in a medium frying pan (skillet). Pour in batter to cover the base thinly. Cook for 2 minutes until golden, then cook the other side for about 1 minute, until browned. Set aside and make a second pancake.

3 For the filling, beat together the flour, cornflour (cornstarch), sugar and egg. Heat the milk gently in a pan, then beat 2 tablespoons of it into the flour mixture. Transfer to the saucepan and cook gently, stirring constantly until thick. Remove from the heat, cover with baking parchment to prevent a skin forming and leave to cool.

4 Beat the nuts, apricots and ginger into the cooled mixture and put a heaped tablespoonful in the centre of each pancake. Gather and squeeze the edges together to make a bundle. Place in an ovenproof dish in a preheated oven, 180°C/350°F/Gas Mark 4, for 15–20 minutes, until hot but not too brown.

5 To make the sauce, melt the preserve gently with the orange juice, then strain. Return to a clean pan with the orange rind and heat through. Serve with the pancakes.

Ginger & Apricot Alaskas

There is no ice cream in this Alaska but a mixture of apples and apricots poached in orange juice enclosed in meringue.

NUTRITIONAL INFORMATION

Calories	442	Sugars	........77g
Protein	.........7g	Fat	...........9g
Carbohydrate	...83g	Saturates	.......3g

 15 MINS   🕐 10 MINS

SERVES 2

I N G R E D I E N T S

2 slices rich, dark ginger cake,
    about 2 cm/¾ inch thick

1–2 tbsp ginger wine or rum

1 eating apple

6 ready-to-eat dried apricots, chopped

4 tbsp orange juice or water

15 g/½ oz/1 tbsp flaked (slivered) almonds

2 small egg whites

100 g/3½ oz/⅓ cup caster (superfine) sugar

1 Place each slice of ginger cake on an ovenproof plate and sprinkle with the ginger wine or rum.

2 Quarter, core and slice the apple into a small saucepan. Add the chopped apricots and orange juice or water, and simmer over a low heat for about 5 minutes, or until tender.

3 Stir the almonds into the fruit and spoon the mixture equally over the slices of soaked cake, piling it up in the centre.

4 Whisk the egg whites until very stiff and dry, then whisk in the sugar, a little at a time, making sure the meringue has become stiff again before adding any more sugar.

5 Either pipe or spread the meringue over the fruit and cake, making sure that both are completely covered.

6 Place in a preheated oven, 200°C/ 400°F/Gas Mark 6, for 4–5 minutes, until golden brown. Serve hot.

VARIATION

A slice of vanilla, coffee or chocolate ice cream can be placed on the fruit before adding the meringue, but this must be done at the last minute and the dessert must be eaten immediately after it is removed from the oven.

Traditional Apple Pie

This apple pie has a double crust and can be served either hot or cold.
The apples can be flavoured with other spices or grated citrus rind.

NUTRITIONAL INFORMATION

Calories 577	Sugars 36g	
Protein 6g	Fat 28g	
Carbohydrate ...80g	Saturates 9g	

 55 MINS   🕐 50 MINS

SERVES 6

I N G R E D I E N T S

750 g–1 kg/1 lb 10 oz–2 lb 4 oz cooking
apples, peeled, cored and sliced

about 125 g/4½ oz/generous ½ cup brown
or white sugar, plus extra for sprinkling

½–1 tsp ground cinnamon, mixed spice
(apple spice) or ground ginger

1–2 tbsp water

SHORTCRUST PASTRY
(PIE DOUGH)

350 g/12 oz/3 cups plain (all-purpose) flour

pinch of salt

90 g/3 oz/6 tbsp butter or margarine

90 g/3 oz/⅓ cup white vegetable
fat (shortening)

about 6 tbsp cold water

beaten egg or milk, for glazing

1 To make the pastry (pie dough), sift the flour and salt into a mixing bowl. Add the butter or margarine and shortening and rub in with the fingertips until the mixture resembles fine breadcrumbs. Add the water and gather the mixture together into a dough. Wrap the dough and chill for 30 minutes.

2 Roll out almost two-thirds of the pastry (pie dough) thinly and use to line a 20–23 cm/8–9 inch deep pie plate or shallow pie tin (pan).

3 Mix the apples with the sugar and spice and pack into the pastry case (pie shell); the filling can come up above the rim. Add the water if liked, particularly if the apples are a dry variety.

4 Roll out the remaining pastry (pie dough) to form a lid. Dampen the edges of the pie rim with water and position the lid, pressing the edges firmly together. Trim and crimp the edges.

5 Use the trimmings to cut out leaves or other shapes to decorate the top of the pie, dampen and attach. Glaze the top of the pie with beaten egg or milk, make 1–2 slits in the top and put the pie on a baking sheet (cookie sheet).

6 Bake in a preheated oven, 220°C/425°F/Gas Mark 7, for 20 minutes, then reduce the temperature to 180°C/350°F/Gas Mark 4 and cook for about 30 minutes, until the pastry is a light golden brown. Serve hot or cold, sprinkled with sugar.

Carrot Dessert

This makes an impressive dinner-party dessert. It is best served warm, with cream and can be made well in advance because it freezes well.

NUTRITIONAL INFORMATION

Calories 509	Sugars 54g	
Protein 8g	Fat 30g	
Carbohydrate ...55g	Saturates 19g	

10 MINS   1 HOUR

SERVES 6

I N G R E D I E N T S

1.5 kg/3 lb 5 oz carrots

10 tbsp ghee

600 ml/1 pint/2½ pints milk

175 ml/6 fl oz/¾ cup evaporated milk or
   khoya

10 whole cardamoms, peeled and crushed

8–10 tbsp sugar

TO DECORATE

25 g/1 oz/¼ cup pistachio nuts, chopped

2 leaves varq (silver leaf) (optional)

1 Rinse, peel and carefully grate the carrots.

2 Heat the ghee in a large, heavy saucepan.

3 Add the grated carrots to the ghee and stir-fry for 15–20 minutes, or until the moisture from the carrots has evaporated and the carrots have darkened in colour.

4 Add the milk, evaporated milk or khoya, cardamoms and sugar to the carrot mixture and continue to stir-fry for a further 30–35 minutes, until it is a rich brownish-red colour.

5 Transfer the carrot mixture to a large shallow dish.

6 Decorate with the pistachio nuts and varq, if using, and serve at once.

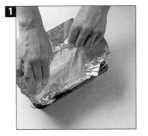

COOK'S TIP

Pure ghee is best for this dessert, as it is rather special and tastes better. However, if you are trying to limit your fat intake, use vegetable ghee instead.

Baked Semolina Pudding

Succulent plums simmered in orange juice and mixed spice (apple spice) complement this rich and creamy semolina pudding perfectly.

NUTRITIONAL INFORMATION

Calories 304	Sugars 32g
Protein 9g	Fat 12g
Carbohydrate ...43g	Saturates 4g

5 MINS   45 MINS

SERVES 4

I N G R E D I E N T S

25 g/1 oz/2 tbsp butter or margarine

600 ml/1 pint/2½ cups milk

finely pared rind and juice of 1 orange

60 g/2 oz/⅓ cup semolina

pinch of grated nutmeg

25 g/1 oz/2 tbsp caster (superfine) sugar

1 egg, beaten

T O   S E R V E

knob of butter

grated nutmeg

S P I C E D   P L U M S

225 g/8 oz plums, halved and stoned (pitted)

150 ml/¼ pint/⅔ cup orange juice

25 g/1 oz/2 tbsp caster (superfine) sugar

½ tsp ground mixed spice (apple spice)

1 Grease a 1 litre/1¾ pint/4 cup ovenproof dish with a little of the butter or margarine. Put the milk, the remaining butter or margarine and the orange rind in a saucepan. Sprinkle in the semolina and heat until boiling, stirring constantly. Simmer gently for 2–3 minutes. Remove from the heat.

2 Add the nutmeg, orange juice and sugar to the semolina mixture, stirring well. Add the egg and stir to mix.

3 Transfer the mixture to the prepared dish and bake in a preheated oven, 190°C/375°F/Gas Mark 5, for about 30 minutes, until lightly browned.

4 To make the spiced plums, put the plums, orange juice, sugar and spice into a saucepan and simmer gently for about 10 minutes, until just tender. Set aside to cool slightly.

5 Top the semolina pudding with a knob of butter and grated nutmeg and serve with the spiced plums.

Cherry Clafoutis

This is a hot dessert that is simple and quick to put together. Try the batter with other fruits. Apricots and plums are particularly delicious.

NUTRITIONAL INFORMATION

Calories 261   Sugars 24g
Protein . . . . .10g   Fat 6g
Carbohydrate . . .40g   Saturates 3g

10 MINS   40 MINS

SERVES 6

I N G R E D I E N T S

125 g/4½ oz/1 cup plain (all-
   purpose) flour

4 eggs, lightly beaten

2 tbsp caster (superfine) sugar

pinch of salt

600 ml/1 pint/2½ cups milk

butter, for greasing

500 g/1 lb 2 oz black cherries,
fresh or canned, stoned (pitted)

3 tbsp brandy

1 tbsp sugar, to decorate

1 Sift the flour into a large mixing bowl. Make a well in the centre and add the eggs, sugar and salt. Gradually, draw in the flour from around the edges and whisk.

2 Pour in the milk and whisk the batter thoroughly until very smooth.

3 Thoroughly grease a 1.75 litre/3 pint/7½ cup ovenproof serving dish with butter and pour in about half of the batter.

4 Spoon over the cherries and pour the remaining batter over the top. Sprinkle the brandy over the batter.

5 Bake in a preheated oven, 180°C/ 350°F/Gas Mark 4, for 40 minutes, until risen and golden.

6 Remove from the oven and sprinkle over the sugar just before serving. Serve warm.

Sweet Saffron Rice

This is a traditional Indian dessert, which is quick and easy to make and looks very impressive, especially decorated with pistachio nuts and varq.

NUTRITIONAL INFORMATION

Calories 460	Sugars 57g
Protein 4g	Fat 9g
Carbohydrate . . .97g	Saturates 5g

 5 MINS   35 MINS

SERVES 4

I N G R E D I E N T S

200 g/7 oz/1 cup basmati rice

200 g/7 oz/1 cup sugar

1 pinch saffron strands

300 ml/½ pint/1¼ cups water

2 tbsp vegetable ghee

3 cloves

3 cardamoms

25 g/1 oz/2 tbsp sultanas (golden raisins)

TO DECORATE

a few pistachio nuts (optional)

varq (silver leaf) (optional)

1 Rinse the rice twice and bring to the boil in a saucepan of water, stirring constantly. Remove the pan from the heat when the rice is half-cooked, drain the rice thoroughly and set aside.

2 In a separate saucepan, boil the sugar and saffron in the water, stirring constantly, until the syrup thickens. Set the syrup aside until required.

3 In another saucepan, heat the ghee, cloves and cardamoms, stirring occasionally. Remove the pan from the heat.

4 Return the rice to a low heat and stir in the sultanas (golden raisins).

5 Pour the syrup over the rice mixture and stir to mix.

6 Pour the ghee mixture over the rice and simmer over a low heat for about 10–15 minutes. Check to see whether the rice is cooked. If it is not, add a little boiling water, cover and continue to simmer until tender.

7 Serve warm, decorated with pistachio nuts and varq (silver leaf), if desired.

COOK'S TIP

Basmati rice is the 'prince of rices' and comes from the Himalayan foothills. Its name means fragrant and it has a superb texture and flavour.

Fruit Brûlée

This is a cheat's brûlée, in that yogurt is used to cover a base of fruit, before being sprinkled with sugar and grilled (broiled).

NUTRITIONAL INFORMATION

Calories	311	Sugars	........48g
Protein	.........7g	Fat	..........11g
Carbohydrate	...48g	Saturates	.......7g

🍲 1¼ HOURS   🕐 15 MINS

SERVES 4

INGREDIENTS

4 plums, stoned (pitted) and sliced

2 cooking apples, peeled and sliced

1 tsp ground ginger

600 ml/1 pint/2½ cups Greek-style yogurt

2 tbsp icing (confectioners') sugar, sifted

1 tsp almond essence (extract)

75 g/2¾ oz/⅓ cup demerara
    (brown crystal) sugar

1 Put the plums and apples in a saucepan with 2 tablespoons of water and cook for 7–10 minutes, until tender, but not mushy. Set aside to cool, then stir in the ginger.

2 Using a slotted spoon, spoon the mixture into the base of a shallow serving dish.

COOK'S TIP

Use any variety of fruit, such as mixed berries or mango pieces, for this dessert, but in that case, do not poach them.

3 Mix the yogurt, icing (confectioners') sugar and almond essence (extract) and spoon on to the fruit to cover.

4 Sprinkle the demerara (brown crystal) sugar over the top of the yogurt and cook under a hot grill (broiler) for 3–4 minutes, or until the sugar has dissolved and formed a crust.

5 Leave to chill in the refrigerator for 1 hour and serve.

Rhubarb & Orange Crumble

A mixture of rhubarb and apples flavoured with orange rind, brown sugar and spices and topped with a crunchy crumble topping.

NUTRITIONAL INFORMATION

Calories 516	Sugars 45g
Protein 6g	Fat 22g
Carbohydrate . . .77g	Saturates 4g

15 MINS   45 MINS

SERVES 6

INGREDIENTS

500 g/1 lb 2 oz rhubarb

500 g/1 lb 2 oz cooking apples

grated rind and juice of 1 orange

½–1 tsp ground cinnamon

about 90 g/3 oz/scant ½ cup light soft brown sugar

CRUMBLE

225 g/8 oz/2 cups plain (all-purpose) flour

125 g/4½ oz/½ cup butter or margarine

125 g/4½ oz/generous ½ cup light soft brown sugar

40–60 g/1½–2 oz/⅓–½ cup toasted chopped hazelnuts

2 tbsp demerara (brown crystal) sugar (optional)

VARIATION

Other flavourings, such as 60 g/2 oz/ generous ¼ cup chopped stem (preserved) ginger, can be added either to the fruit or the crumb mixture. Any fruit, or mixtures of fruit can be topped with crumble.

1 Cut the rhubarb into 2.5 cm/1 inch lengths and place in a large saucepan.

2 Peel, core and slice the apples and add to the rhubarb, together with the grated orange rind and juice. Bring to the boil, lower the heat and simmer for 2–3 minutes, until the fruit begins to soften.

3 Add the cinnamon and sugar to taste and turn the mixture into an ovenproof dish, so it is not more than two-thirds full.

4 Sift the flour into a bowl and rub in the butter or margarine until the mixture resembles fine breadcrumbs (this can be done by hand or in a food processor). Stir in the sugar, followed by the nuts.

5 Spoon the crumble mixture evenly over the fruit in the dish and level the top. Sprinkle with demerara (brown crystal) sugar, if liked.

6 Cook in a preheated oven, 200°C/ 400°F/Gas Mark 6, for 30–40 minutes, until the topping is browned. Serve hot or cold.

Sweet Carrot Halva

This nutritious dessert is flavoured with spices, nuts and raisins. The nutritional information does not include serving with cream.

NUTRITIONAL INFORMATION

Calories	284	Sugars	........33g
Protein	.........7g	Fat	..........14g
Carbohydrate	...34g	Saturates	.......3g

 10 MINS   55 MINS

SERVES 6

I N G R E D I E N T S

750 g/1 lb 10 oz carrots, grated

700 ml/1¼ pints/3 cups milk

1 cinnamon stick or piece of
  cassia bark (optional)

4 tbsp vegetable ghee or oil

60 g/2 oz/¼ cup granulated sugar

25 g/1 oz/¼ cup unsalted
  pistachio nuts, chopped

25–50 g/1–1¾ oz/¼–½ cup blanched
  almonds, flaked (slivered) or chopped

60 g/2 oz/⅓ cup seedless raisins

8 cardamom pods, split and seeds removed
  and crushed

thick cream, to serve

1 Put the grated carrots, milk and cinnamon or cassia, if using, into a large, heavy-based saucepan and bring to the boil. Reduce the heat to very low and simmer, uncovered, for about 35–40 minutes, or until the mixture is thick (with no milk remaining). Stir the mixture frequently during cooking to prevent it from sticking.

2 Remove and discard the cinnamon or cassia. Heat the ghee or oil in a non-stick frying pan, add the carrot mixture and stir-fry over a medium heat for about 5 minutes, or until the carrots take on a glossy sheen.

3 Add the sugar, pistachios, almonds, raisins and crushed cardamom seeds, mix thoroughly and continue frying for a further 3–4 minutes, stirring frequently. Serve warm or cold with thick cream.

COOK'S TIP

The quickest and easiest way to grate this quantity of carrots is by using a food processor fitted with the appropriate blade. This mixture may be prepared ahead of time and reheated in the microwave when required.

Spun Sugar Pears

Whole pears are poached in a Madeira syrup in the microwave, then served with a delicate spun sugar surround.

NUTRITIONAL INFORMATION

Calories	166	Sugars	........41g
Protein	........0.3g	Fat	...........0g
Carbohydrate	...41g	Saturates	......0g

  20 MINS   35 MINS

SERVES 4

I N G R E D I E N T S

150 ml/¼ pint/⅔ cup water

150 ml/¼ pint/⅔ cup sweet Madeira wine

125 g/4½ oz/½ cup caster (superfine) sugar

2 tbsp lime juice

4 ripe pears, peeled, stalks left on

sprigs of fresh mint to decorate

S P U N   S U G A R

125 g/4½ oz/½ cup caster (superfine) sugar

3 tbsp water

1 Mix the water, Madeira, sugar and lime juice in a large bowl. Cover and cook on HIGH power for 3 minutes. Stir well until the sugar dissolves.

2 Peel the pears and cut a slice from the base of each one so they stand upright.

3 Add the pears to the bowl, spooning the wine syrup over them. Cover and cook on HIGH power for about 10 minutes, turning the pears over every few minutes, until they are tender. The cooking time may vary slightly depending on the ripeness of the pears. Leave to cool, covered, in the syrup.

4 Remove the cooled pears from the syrup and set aside on serving plates. Cook the syrup, uncovered, on HIGH power for about 15 minutes until reduced by half and thickened slightly. Leave to stand for 5 minutes. Spoon over the pears.

5 To make the spun sugar, mix together the sugar and water in a bowl. Cook, uncovered, on HIGH power for 1½ minutes. Stir until the sugar has dissolved completely. Continue to cook on HIGH power for about 5–6 minutes more until the sugar has caramelized.

6 Wait for the caramel bubbles to subside and leave to stand for 2 minutes. Dip a teaspoon in the caramel and spin sugar around each pear in a circular motion. Serve immediately, decorated with sprigs of mint.

COOK'S TIP

Keep checking the caramel during the last few minutes of the cooking time, as it will change colour quite quickly and continue to cook for several minutes after removing from the microwave oven.

Tropical Salad

Paw-paws (papayas) are ready to eat when they yield to gentle pressure.
Serve in the shells of baby pineapples for a stunning effect.

NUTRITIONAL INFORMATION

Calories	69	Sugars	........13g
Protein	.........1g	Fat	..........0.3g
Carbohydrate	...14g	Saturates	......0g

 10 MINS 0 MINS

SERVES 8

I N G R E D I E N T S

1 paw-paw (papaya)

2 tbsp fresh orange juice

3 tbsp rum

2 bananas

2 guavas

1 small pineapple or 2 baby
   pineapples

2 passion-fruit

pineapple leaves to decorate

1 Cut the paw-paw (papaya) in half and remove the seeds. Peel and slice the flesh into a bowl.

2 Pour over the orange juice together with the rum.

3 Slice the bananas, peel and slice the guavas, and add both to the bowl.

4 Cut the top and base from the pineapple, then cut off the skin.

5 Slice the pineapple flesh, discard the core, cut into pieces and add to the bowl.

6 Halve the passion-fruit, scoop out the flesh with a teaspoon, add to the bowl and stir well to mix.

7 Spoon the salad into glass bowls and decorate with pineapple leaves.

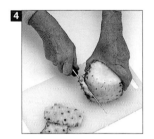

COOK'S TIP

Guavas have a heavenly smell when ripe – their scent will fill a whole room. They should give to gentle pressure when ripe, and their skins should be yellow. The canned varieties are very good and have a pink tinge to the flesh.

Orange Syllabub

A zesty, creamy whip made from yogurt and milk with a hint of orange, served with light and luscious sweet sponge cakes.

NUTRITIONAL INFORMATION

Calories 464   Sugars 74g
Protein ....22g   Fat 5g
Carbohydrate ...89g   Saturates 2g

 1½ HOURS   10 MINS

SERVES 4

I N G R E D I E N T S

4 oranges

600 ml/1 pint/2½ cups low-fat natural yogurt

6 tbsp low-fat skimmed milk powder

4 tbsp caster (superfine) sugar

1 tbsp grated orange rind

4 tbsp orange juice

2 egg whites

fresh orange zest to decorate

SPONGE HEARTS

2 eggs, size 2

90 g/3 oz/6 tbsp caster (superfine) sugar

40 g/1½ oz/6 tbsp plain (all-purpose) flour

40 g/1½ oz/6 tbsp wholemeal (whole wheat) flour

1 tbsp hot water

1 tsp icing (confectioners') sugar

1 Slice off the tops and bottoms of the oranges and the skin. Then cut out the segments, removing the zest and membranes between each one. Divide the orange segments between 4 dessert glasses, then chill.

2 In a mixing bowl, combine the yogurt, milk powder, sugar, orange rind and juice. Cover and chill for 1 hour. Whisk the egg whites until stiff, then fold into the yogurt mixture. Pile on to the orange slices and chill for an hour. Decorate with fresh orange rind and sponge hearts.

3 To make the sponge hearts, line a 15 × 25 cm/6 × 10 inch baking tin (pan) with baking parchment. Whisk the eggs and caster (superfine) sugar until thick and pale. Sieve, then fold in the flours using a large metal spoon, adding the hot water at the same time.

4 Pour into the tin (pan) and bake in a preheated oven at 220°C/425°F/Gas Mark 7 for 9–10 minutes until golden and firm to the touch.

5 Turn on to a sheet of baking parchment. Using a 5 cm/2 inch heart-shaped cutter, stamp out hearts. Transfer to a wire rack to cool. Lightly dust with icing (confectioners') sugar before serving with the syllabub.

New Age Spotted Dick

This is a deliciously moist low-fat pudding. The sauce is in the centre of the pudding, and will spill out when the pudding is cut.

NUTRITIONAL INFORMATION

Calories	...529	Sugars	...41g
Protein	...9g	Fat	...31g
Carbohydrate	...58g	Saturates	...4g

 25 MINS   1¼ HOURS

SERVES 6–8

INGREDIENTS

125 g/4½ oz/¾ cup raisins

125 ml/4 fl oz/generous ½ cup corn oil, plus a little for brushing

125 g/4½ oz/generous ½ cup caster (superfine) sugar

25 g/1 oz/¼ cup ground almonds

2 eggs, lightly beaten

175 g/6 oz/1½ cups self-raising flour

SAUCE

60 g/2 oz/½ cup walnuts, chopped

60 g/2 oz/½ cup ground almonds

300 ml/½ pint/1¼ cups semi-skimmed milk

4 tbsp granulated sugar

1 Put the raisins in a saucepan with 125 ml/4 fl oz/½ cup water. Bring to the boil, then remove from the heat. Leave to steep for 10 minutes, then drain.

2 Whisk together the oil, sugar and ground almonds until thick and syrupy; this will need about 8 minutes of beating (on medium speed if using an electric whisk).

3 Add the eggs, one at a time, beating well after each addition. Combine the flour and raisins. Stir into the mixture. Brush a 1 litre/1¾ pint/4 cup pudding basin with oil, or line with baking parchment.

4 Put all the sauce ingredients into a saucepan. Bring to the boil, stir and simmer for 10 minutes.

5 Transfer the sponge mixture to the greased basin and pour on the hot sauce. Place on a baking tray (cookie sheet).

6 Bake in a preheated oven at 170°C/340°F/Gas Mark 3½ for about 1 hour. Lay a piece of baking parchment across the top if it starts to brown too fast.

7 Leave to cool for 2–3 minutes in the basin before turning out on to a serving plate.

COOK'S TIP

Always soak raisins before baking them, as they retain their moisture nicely and you taste the flavour of them instead of biting on a dried-out raisin.

Red Fruits with Frothy Sauce

A colourful combination of soft fruits, served with a marshmallow sauce, is an ideal dessert when summer fruits are in season.

NUTRITIONAL INFORMATION

Calories 219	Sugars 55g
Protein 2g	Fat 0.3g
Carbohydrate . . .55g	Saturates 0g

1¼ HOURS   20 MINS

SERVES 4

I N G R E D I E N T S

225 g/8 oz redcurrants, washed and trimmed, thawed if frozen

225 g/8 oz cranberries

75 g/2¾ oz light muscovado sugar

200 ml/7 fl oz/¾ cup unsweetened apple juice

1 cinnamon stick, broken

300 g/10½ oz small strawberries, washed, hulled and halved

S A U C E

225 g/8 oz raspberries, thawed if frozen

2 tbsp fruit cordial

100 g/3½ oz marshmallows

1 Place the redcurrants, cranberries and sugar in a saucepan. Pour in the apple juice and add the cinnamon stick. Bring the mixture to the boil and simmer gently for 10 minutes until the fruit is soft.

COOK'S TIP

This sauce is delicious poured over low-fat ice cream. For an extra-colourful sauce, replace the raspberries with an assortment of summer berries.

2 Stir the strawberries into the fruit mixture and mix well. Transfer the mixture to a bowl, cover and leave to chill in the refrigerator for about 1 hour. Remove and discard the cinnamon stick.

3 Just before serving, make the sauce. Place the raspberries and fruit cordial in a small saucepan, bring to the boil and simmer for 2–3 minutes until the fruit is just beginning to soften. Stir the marshmallows into the raspberry mixture and heat through, stirring, until the marshmallows begin to melt.

4 Transfer the fruit salad to serving bowls. Spoon over the raspberry and marshmallow sauce and serve.

Paper-Thin Fruit Pies

The extra-crisp pastry cases, filled with slices of fruit and glazed with apricot jam, are best served hot with low-fat custard.

NUTRITIONAL INFORMATION

Calories 158	Sugars 12g
Protein 2g	Fat 10g
Carbohydrate ...14g	Saturates 2g

20 MINS   15 MINS

SERVES 4

INGREDIENTS

1 medium eating (dessert) apple

1 medium ripe pear

2 tbsp lemon juice

60 g/2 oz low-fat spread

4 rectangular sheets of filo pastry, thawed if frozen

2 tbsp low-sugar apricot jam

1 tbsp unsweetened orange juice

1 tbsp finely chopped natural pistachio nuts, shelled

2 tsp icing (confectioners') sugar, for dusting

low-fat custard, to serve

1 Preheat the oven to 200°C/400°F/Gas Mark 6. Core and thinly slice the apple and pear and toss them in the lemon juice.

2 Over a low heat, gently melt the low-fat spread.

3 Cut the sheets of pastry into 4 and cover with a clean, damp tea towel (dish cloth). Brush 4 non-stick Yorkshire pudding tins (large muffin pans), measuring 10 cm/4 inch across, with a little of the low-fat spread.

4 Working on each pie separately, brush 4 sheets of pastry with low-fat spread. Press a small sheet of pastry into the base of one tin (pan). Arrange the other sheets of pastry on top at slightly different angles. Repeat with the other sheets of pastry to make another 3 pies.

5 Arrange the apple and pear slices alternately in the centre of each pastry case and lightly crimp the edges of the pastry of each pie.

6 Mix the jam and orange juice together until smooth and brush over the fruit. Bake for 12–15 minutes. Sprinkle with the pistachio nuts, dust lightly with icing (confectioners') sugar and serve hot with low-fat custard.

VARIATION

Other combinations of fruit are equally delicious. Try peach and apricot, raspberry and apple, or pineapple and mango.

Tuscan Pudding

These baked mini-ricotta puddings are delicious served warm or chilled and will keep in the refrigerator for 3–4 days.

NUTRITIONAL INFORMATION

Calories ....293 Sugars 28g
Protein ....9g Fat 17g
Carbohydrate ...28g Saturates 9g

 20 MINS   15 MINS

SERVES 4

I N G R E D I E N T S

15 g/½ oz/1 tbsp butter

75 g/2¾ oz mixed dried fruit

250 g/9 oz ricotta cheese

3 egg yolks

50 g/1¾ oz caster (superfine) sugar

1 tsp cinnamon

finely grated rind of 1 orange,
   plus extra to decorate

crème fraîche (soured cream), to serve

1 Lightly grease 4 mini pudding basins or ramekin dishes with the butter.

2 Put the dried fruit in a bowl and cover with warm water. Leave to soak for 10 minutes.

COOK'S TIP

Crème fraîche (soured cream) has a slightly sour, nutty taste and is very thick. It is suitable for cooking, but has the same fat content as double (heavy) cream. It can be made by stirring cultured buttermilk into double (heavy) cream and refrigerating overnight.

3 Beat the ricotta cheese with the egg yolks in a bowl. Stir in the caster (superfine) sugar, cinnamon and orange rind and mix to combine.

4 Drain the dried fruit in a sieve set over a bowl. Mix the drained fruit with the ricotta cheese mixture.

5 Spoon the mixture into the basins or ramekin dishes.

6 Bake in a preheated oven, at 180°C/350°F/Gas Mark 4, for 15 minutes. The tops should be firm to the touch but not brown.

7 Decorate the puddings with grated orange rind. Serve warm or chilled with a dollop of crème fraîche (soured cream), if liked.

Mascarpone Cheesecake

The mascarpone gives this baked cheesecake a wonderfully tangy flavour. Ricotta cheese could be used as an alternative.

NUTRITIONAL INFORMATION

Calories 327	Sugars 25g	
Protein 9g	Fat 18g	
Carbohydrate ...33g	Saturates 11g	

15 MINS   50 MINS

SERVES 8

INGREDIENTS

50 g/1¾ oz/1½ tbsp unsalted butter

150 g/5½ oz ginger biscuits
   (cookies), crushed

25 g/1 oz stem ginger (candied), chopped

500 g/1 lb 2 oz mascarpone cheese

finely grated rind and juice of 2 lemons

100 g/3½ oz caster (superfine) sugar

2 large eggs, separated

fruit coulis (see Cook's Tip), to serve

1 Grease and line the base of a 25 cm/10 inch spring-form cake tin (pan) or loose-bottomed tin (pan).

2 Melt the butter in a pan and stir in the crushed biscuits (cookies) and chopped ginger. Use the mixture to line the tin (pan), pressing the mixture about 6 mm/¼ inch up the sides.

COOK'S TIP

Fruit coulis can be made by cooking 400 g/14 oz fruit, such as blueberries, for 5 minutes with 2 tablespoons of water. Sieve the mixture, then stir in 1 tablespoon (or more to taste) of sifted icing (confectioners') sugar. Leave to cool before serving.

3 Beat together the cheese, lemon rind and juice, sugar and egg yolks until quite smooth.

4 Whisk the egg whites until they are stiff and fold into the cheese and lemon mixture.

5 Pour the mixture into the tin (pan) and bake in a preheated oven, at 180°C/350°F/Gas Mark 4, for 35–45 minutes until just set. Don't worry if it cracks or sinks – this is quite normal.

6 Leave the cheesecake in the tin (pan) to cool. Serve with fruit coulis (see Cook's Tip).

Zabaglione

This well-known dish is really a light but rich egg mousse flavoured with Marsala.

NUTRITIONAL INFORMATION

Calories	158	Sugars	........29g
Protein	.........1g	Fat	..........1g
Carbohydrate	...29g	Saturates	.....0.2g

 5 MINS   15 MINS

SERVES 4

INGREDIENTS

5 egg yolks

100 g/3½ oz caster (superfine) sugar

150 ml/¼ pint/⅔ cup Marsala or
  sweet sherry

amaretti biscuits (cookies), to serve
  (optional)

1 Place the egg yolks in a large mixing bowl.

2 Add the caster (superfine) sugar to the egg yolks and whisk until the mixture is thick and very pale and has doubled in volume.

3 Place the bowl containing the egg yolk and sugar mixture over a saucepan of gently simmering water.

4 Add the Marsala or sherry to the egg yolk and sugar mixture and continue whisking until the foam mixture becomes warm. This process may take as long as 10 minutes.

5 Pour the mixture, which should be frothy and light, into 4 wine glasses.

6 Serve the zabaglione warm with fresh fruit or amaretti biscuits (cookies), if you wish.

Quick Tiramisu

This quick version of one of the most popular Italian desserts is ready in minutes.

NUTRITIONAL INFORMATION

Calories	387	Sugars	........17g
Protein	.........9g	Fat	..........28g
Carbohydrate	...22g	Saturates	......15g

  15 MINS 0 MINS

SERVES 4

I N G R E D I E N T S

225 g/8 oz/1 cup Mascarpone or full-fat
soft cheese

1 egg, separated

2 tbsp natural yogurt

2 tbsp caster (superfine) sugar

2 tbsp dark rum

2 tbsp strong black coffee

8 sponge fingers (lady fingers)

2 tbsp grated dark chocolate

1 Put the cheese in a large bowl, add the egg yolk and yogurt and beat until smooth.

2 Whisk the egg white until stiff but not dry, then whisk in the sugar and carefully fold into the cheese mixture.

3 Spoon half of the mixture into 4 sundae glasses.

4 Mix together the rum and coffee in a shallow dish. Dip the sponge fingers (lady-fingers) into the rum mixture, break them in half, or into smaller pieces if necessary, and divide among the glasses.

5 Stir any remaining coffee mixture into the remaining cheese and spoon over the top.

6 Sprinkle with grated chocolate. Serve immediately or chill until required.

COOK'S TIP

Mascarpone is an Italian soft cream cheese made from cow's milk. It has a rich, silky smooth texture and a deliciously creamy flavour. It can be eaten as it is with fresh fruits or flavoured with coffee or chocolate.

Peaches in White Wine

A very simple but incredibly pleasing dessert, which is especially good for a dinner party on a hot summer day.

NUTRITIONAL INFORMATION

Calories 89	Sugars 14g	
Protein 1g	Fat 0g	
Carbohydrate ...14g	Saturates 0g	

 1¼ HOURS   0 MINS

SERVES 4

INGREDIENTS

4 large ripe peaches

2 tbsp icing (confectioners') sugar, sifted

1 orange

200 ml/7 fl oz/¾ cup medium or sweet
  white wine, chilled

1 Using a sharp knife, halve the peaches, remove the stones (pits) and discard them. Peel the peaches, if you prefer. Slice the peaches into thin wedges.

2 Place the peach wedges in a serving bowl and sprinkle over the sugar.

3 Using a sharp knife, pare the rind from the orange. Cut the orange rind into matchsticks, place them in a bowl of cold water and set aside.

4 Squeeze the juice from the orange and pour over the peaches together with the wine.

5 Let the peaches marinate and chill in the refrigerator for at least 1 hour.

6 Remove the orange rind from the cold water and pat dry with paper towels.

7 Garnish the peaches with the strips of orange rind and serve immediately.

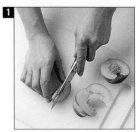

Peaches & Mascarpone

If you prepare these in advance, all you have to do is pop the peaches on the barbecue (grill) when you are ready to serve them.

NUTRITIONAL INFORMATION

Calories 301	Sugars 24g	
Protein 6g	Fat 20g	
Carbohydrate . . .24g	Saturates 9g	

10 MINS   10 MINS

SERVES 4

INGREDIENTS

4 peaches

175 g/6 oz mascarpone cheese

40 g/1½ oz pecan or walnuts, chopped

1 tsp sunflower oil

4 tbsp maple syrup

1 Cut the peaches in half and remove the stones. If you are preparing this recipe in advance, press the peach halves together again and wrap them in cling film (plastic wrap) until required.

2 Mix the mascarpone and pecan or walnuts together in a small bowl until well combined. Leave to chill in the refrigerator until required.

VARIATION

You can use nectarines instead of peaches for this recipe. Remember to choose ripe but firm fruit which won't go soft and mushy when it is barbecued (grilled). Prepare the nectarines in the same way as the peaches and barbecue (grill) for 5–10 minutes.

3 To serve, brush the peaches with a little oil and place on a rack set over medium hot coals. Barbecue (grill) for 5–10 minutes, turning once, until hot.

4 Transfer the peaches to a serving dish and top with the mascarpone mixture.

5 Drizzle the maple syrup over the peaches and mascarpone filling and serve at once.

Sweet Mascarpone Mousse

A sweet cream cheese dessert that complements the tartness of fresh summer fruits rather well.

NUTRITIONAL INFORMATION

Calories 542	Sugars 31g	
Protein 14g	Fat 41g	
Carbohydrate ...31g	Saturates 24g	

 1½ HOURS 0 MINS

SERVES 4

INGREDIENTS

450 g/1 lb mascarpone cheese

100 g/3½ oz caster (superfine) sugar

4 egg yolks

400 g/14 oz frozen summer fruits, such as
    raspberries and redcurrants

redcurrants, to garnish

amaretti biscuits (cookies), to serve

1 Place the mascarpone cheese in a large mixing bowl. Using a wooden spoon, beat the mascarpone cheese until quite smooth.

2 Stir the egg yolks and sugar into the mascarpone cheese, mixing well. Leave the mixture to chill in the refrigerator for about 1 hour.

3 Spoon a layer of the mascarpone mixture into the bottom of 4 individual serving dishes. Spoon a layer of the summer fruits on top. Repeat the layers in the same order, reserving some of the mascarpone mixture for the top.

4 Leave the mousses to chill in the refrigerator for about 20 minutes. The fruits should still be slightly frozen.

5 Serve the mascarpone mousses with amaretti biscuits (cookies).

Panettone & Strawberries

Panettone is a sweet Italian bread. It is delicious toasted, and when it is topped with marscapone and strawberries it makes a sumptuous dessert.

NUTRITIONAL INFORMATION

Calories 227	Sugars 11g	
Protein 5g	Fat 13g	
Carbohydrate ...19g	Saturates 8g	

 35 MINS   🕐 2 MINS

SERVES 4

INGREDIENTS

225 g/8 oz strawberries

25 g/1 oz caster (superfine) sugar

6 tbsp Marsala wine

½ tsp ground cinnamon

4 slices panettone

4 tbsp mascarpone cheese

1 Hull and slice the strawberries and place them in a bowl. Add the sugar, Marsala and cinnamon to the strawberries.

2 Toss the strawberries in the sugar and cinnamon mixture until they are well coated. Leave to chill in the refrigerator for at least 30 minutes.

3 When ready to serve, transfer the slices of panettone to a rack set over medium hot coals. Barbecue (grill) the panettone for about 1 minute on each side or until golden brown.

4 Carefully remove the panettone from the barbecue (grill) and transfer to serving plates.

5 Top the panettone with the mascarpone cheese and the marinated strawberries. Serve immediately.

Vanilla Ice Cream

This home-made version of real vanilla ice cream is absolutely delicious and so easy to make. A tutti-frutti variation is also provided.

NUTRITIONAL INFORMATION

Calories 626	Sugars 33g	
Protein 7g	Fat 53g	
Carbohydrate . . .33g	Saturates 31g	

5 MINS   15 MINS

SERVES 6

INGREDIENTS

600 ml/1 pint/2½ cups double
   (heavy) cream

1 vanilla pod

pared rind of 1 lemon

4 eggs, beaten

2 egg yolks

175 g/6 oz caster (superfine) sugar

1 Place the cream in a heavy-based saucepan and heat gently, whisking.

2 Add the vanilla pod, lemon rind, eggs and egg yolks to the pan and heat until the mixture reaches just below boiling point.

3 Reduce the heat and cook for 8–10 minutes, whisking the mixture continuously, until thickened.

VARIATION

For tutti frutti ice cream, soak 100 g/3½ oz mixed dried fruit in 2 tbsp Marsala or sweet sherry for 20 minutes. Follow the method for vanilla ice cream, omitting the vanilla pod, and stir in the Marsala or sherry-soaked fruit in step 6, just before freezing.

4 Stir the sugar into the cream mixture, set aside and leave to cool.

5 Strain the cream mixture through a sieve (strainer).

6 Slit open the vanilla pod, scoop out the tiny black seeds and stir them into the cream.

7 Pour the mixture into a shallow freezing container with a lid and freeze overnight until set. Serve the ice cream when required.

Mango Mousse

This is a light, softly set and tangy mousse, which is perfect for clearing the palate after a meal of mixed flavours.

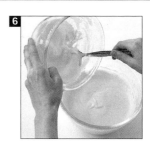

NUTRITIONAL INFORMATION

Calories	346	Sugars	........27g
Protein	.........7g	Fat	..........24g
Carbohydrate	...27g	Saturates	......15g

 40 MINS 0 MINS

SERVES 4

INGREDIENTS

400 g/14 oz can mangoes in syrup

2 pieces stem (preserved) ginger, chopped

200 ml/7 fl oz/1 cup double (heavy) cream

20 g/¾ oz/4 tsp powdered gelatine

2 tbsp hot water

2 egg whites

1½ tbsp light brown sugar

stem (preserved) ginger and lime zest, to decorate

1 Drain the mangoes, reserving the syrup. Blend the mango pieces and ginger in a food processor or blender for 30 seconds, or until smooth.

2 Measure the purée and make up to 300 ml/½ pint/1¼ cups with the reserved mango syrup.

3 In a separate bowl, whip the cream until it forms soft peaks. Fold the mango mixture into the cream until well combined.

4 Dissolve the gelatine in the hot water and leave to cool slightly.

5 Pour the gelatine into the mango mixture in a steady stream, stirring.

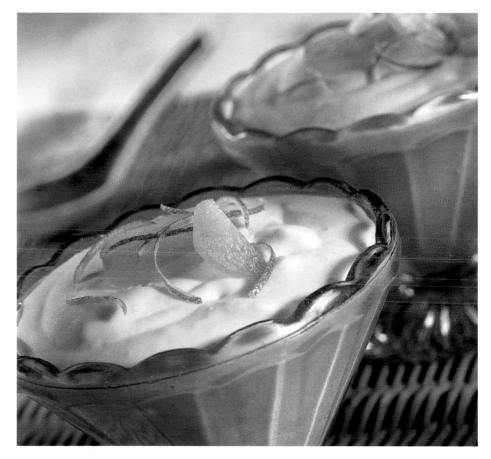

Leave to cool in the refrigerator for 30 minutes, until almost set.

6 Beat the egg whites in a clean bowl until they form soft peaks, then beat in the sugar. Gently fold the egg whites into the mango mixture with a metal spoon.

7 Spoon the mousse into individual serving dishes, decorate with stem (preserved) ginger and lime zest and serve.

COOK'S TIP

The gelatine must be stirred into the mango mixture in a gentle, steady stream to prevent it from setting in lumps when it comes into contact with the cold mixture.

Exotic Fruit Pancakes

These pancakes are filled with an exotic array of tropical fruits. Decorate lavishly with tropical flowers or mint sprigs.

NUTRITIONAL INFORMATION

Calories 382	Sugars 24g	
Protein 7g	Fat 17g	
Carbohydrate ...53g	Saturates 3g	

 40 MINS 35 MINS

SERVES 4

INGREDIENTS

BATTER

125 g/4½ oz/1 cup plain flour

pinch of salt

1 egg

1 egg yolk

300 ml/½ pint/1¼ cups coconut milk

4 tsp vegetable oil, plus oil for frying

FILLING

1 banana

1 paw-paw (papaya)

juice of 1 lime

2 passion fruit

1 mango, peeled, stoned and sliced

4 lychees, stoned and halved

1-2 tbsp honey

flowers or mint sprigs, to decorate

1 Sift the flour and salt into a bowl. Make a well in the centre and add the egg, egg yolk and a little of the coconut milk. Gradually draw the flour into the egg mixture, beating well and slowly adding the remaining coconut milk to make a smooth batter. Stir in the oil. Cover and chill for 30 minutes.

2 Peel and slice the banana and place in a bowl. Peel and slice the paw-paw (papaya), discarding the seeds. Add to the banana with the lime juice and mix well. Cut the passion-fruit in half and scoop out the flesh and seeds into the fruit bowl. Stir in the mango, lychees and honey.

3 Heat a little oil in a 15 cm/6 inch frying pan (skillet). Pour in just enough of the pancake batter to cover the base of the pan and tilt so that it spreads thinly and evenly. Cook until the pancake is just set and the underside is lightly browned, turn and briefly cook the other side. Remove from the pan and keep warm. Repeat with the remaining batter to make a total of 8 pancakes.

4 To serve, place a little of the prepared fruit filling along the centre of each pancake and then roll it into a cone shape. Lay seam-side down on warmed serving plates, decorate with flowers or mint sprigs and serve.

Mango & Passion Fruit Salad

The rich Mascarpone Cream which accompanies the exotic fruit salad gives this Chinese dessert an Italian twist.

NUTRITIONAL INFORMATION

Calories	211	Sugars	. . . . .18g
Protein	. . . . .6g	Fat	. . . . .10g
Carbohydrate	. . .18g	Saturates	. . . . . . .6g

 1¼ HOURS   0 MINS

SERVES 4

I N G R E D I E N T S

1 large mango

2 oranges

4 passion fruit

2 tbsp orange-flavoured liqueur such as Grand Marnier

mint or geranium leaves, to decorate

M A S C A R P O N E   C R E A M

125 g/4½ oz/½ cup Mascarpone cheese

1 tbsp clear honey

4 tbsp thick, natural (unsweetened) yogurt

few drops vanilla flavouring (extract)

1 Using a sharp knife, cut the mango in half lengthwise as close to the stone (pit) as possible. Remove the stone (pit), using a sharp knife.

2 Peel off the mango skin, cut the flesh into slices and place into a large bowl.

3 Peel the oranges, removing all the pith, and cut into segments. Add to the bowl with any juices.

4 Halve the passion fruit, scoop out the flesh and add to the bowl with the orange-flavoured liqueur. Mix together all the ingredients in the bowl.

5 Cover the bowl with cling film (plastic wrap) and chill in the refrigerator for 1 hour. Turn into glass serving dishes.

6 To make the Mascarpone cream, blend the Mascarpone cheese and honey together. Stir in the natural (unsweetened) yogurt and vanilla flavouring (extract) until thoroughly blended.

7 Serve the fruit salad with the Mascarpone cream, decorated with mint or geranium leaves.

COOK'S TIP

Passion fruit are ready to eat when their skins are well dimpled. They are most readily available in the summer. Substitute guava or pineapple for the passion fruit, if you prefer.

Melon & Kiwi Salad

A refreshing fruit salad, ideal to serve after a rich meal. Charentais or cantaloup melons are also good.

NUTRITIONAL INFORMATION

Calories 88   Sugars 17g
Protein . . . . .1g   Fat 0.2g
Carbohydrate . . .17g   Saturates 0g

1¼ HOURS   0 MINS

SERVES 4

INGREDIENTS

½ Galia melon

2 kiwi fruit

125 g/4½ oz/1 cup white (green) seedless grapes

1 paw-paw (papaya), halved

3 tbsp orange-flavoured liqueur such as Cointreau

1 tbsp chopped lemon verbena, lemon balm or mint

sprigs of lemon verbena or Cape gooseberries, to decorate

1 Remove the seeds from the melon, cut into 4 slices and cut away the skin. Cut the flesh into cubes and put into a bowl.

2 Peel the kiwi fruit and cut across into slices. Add to the melon with the white grapes.

3 Remove the seeds from the paw-paw (papaya) and cut off the skin. Slice the flesh thickly and cut into diagonal pieces. Add to the fruit bowl and mix well.

4 Mix together the liqueur and lemon verbena, pour over the fruit and leave for 1 hour, stirring occasionally.

5 Spoon the fruit salad into glasses, pour over the juices and decorate with lemon verbena sprigs or Cape gooseberries.

COOK'S TIP

Lemon balm or sweet balm is a fragrant lemon-scented plant with slightly hairy serrated leaves and a pronounced lemon flavour. Lemon verbena can also be used – this has an even stronger lemon flavour and smooth elongated leaves.

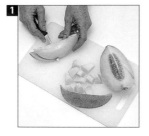

Coconut Cream Moulds

Smooth, creamy and refreshing – these tempting little custards are made with an unusual combination of coconut milk, cream and eggs.

NUTRITIONAL INFORMATION

Calories . . . . . . .288 Sugar 24g
Protein . . . . .4g Fat 20g
Carbohydrate . . .25g Saturates 14g

 10 MINS 45 MINS

SERVES 8

INGREDIENTS

CARAMEL

125 g/4½ oz/½ cup granulated sugar

150 ml/¼ pint/⅔ cup water

CUSTARD

300 ml/½ pint/1¼ cups water

90g/3 oz creamed coconut, chopped

2 eggs

2 egg yolks

1½ tbsp caster (superfine) sugar

300 ml/½ pint/1¼ cups single (light) cream

sliced banana or slivers of fresh pineapple

1-2 tbsp freshly grated or desiccated
   (shredded) coconut

1 Have ready 8 small ovenproof dishes about 150 ml/¼ pint/⅔ cup capacity. To make the caramel, place the granulated sugar and water in a saucepan and heat gently to dissolve the sugar, then boil rapidly, without stirring, until the mixture turns a rich golden brown.

2 Immediately remove the pan from the heat and dip the base into a bowl of cold water in order to stop it cooking further. Quickly, but carefully, pour the caramel into the ovenproof dishes to coat the bases.

3 To make the custard, place the water in the same saucepan, add the coconut and heat, stirring constantly, until the coconut dissolves. Place the eggs, egg yolks and caster (superfine) sugar in a bowl and beat well with a fork. Add the hot coconut milk and stir well to dissolve the sugar. Stir in the cream and strain the mixture into a jug.

4 Arrange the dishes in a roasting tin (pan) and fill with enough cold water to come halfway up the sides of the dishes. Pour the custard mixture into the caramel-lined dishes, cover with greaseproof paper or foil and cook in a preheated oven, 150°C/300°F/Gas Mark 2, for about 40 minutes, or until set.

5 Remove the dishes, set aside to cool and then chill overnight. To serve, run a knife around the edge of each dish and turn out on to a serving plate. Serve with slices of banana or slivers of fresh pineapple sprinkled with freshly grated or desiccated coconut.

Raspberry Fool

This dish is very easy to make and can be prepared in advance and stored in the refrigerator until required.

NUTRITIONAL INFORMATION

Calories	288	Sugars	........19g
Protein	.........4g	Fat	..........22g
Carbohydrate	...19g	Saturates	......14g

1¼ HOURS   0 MINS

SERVES 4

INGREDIENTS

300 g/10½ oz/1⅔ cups fresh raspberries

50 g/1¾ oz/¼ cup icing
   (confectioners') sugar

300 ml/½ pint/1¼ cups crème fraîche,
   plus extra to decorate

½ tsp vanilla essence (extract)

2 egg whites

raspberries and lemon balm leaves,
   to decorate

1 Put the raspberries and icing (confectioners') sugar in a food processor or blender and process until smooth. Alternatively, press through a strainer with the back of a spoon.

2 Reserve 1 tablespoon per portion of crème fraîche for decorating.

3 Put the vanilla essence (extract) and remaining crème fraîche in a bowl and stir in the raspberry mixture.

4 Whisk the egg whites in a separate mixing bowl until stiff peaks form. Gently fold the egg whites into the raspberry mixture using a metal spoon, until fully incorporated.

5 Spoon the raspberry fool into individual serving dishes and chill for at least 1 hour. Decorate with the reserved crème fraîche, raspberries and lemon balm leaves and serve.

COOK'S TIP

Although this dessert is best made with fresh raspberries in season, an acceptable result can be achieved with frozen raspberries, which are available from most supermarkets.

Frozen Citrus Soufflés

These delicious desserts are a refreshing way to end a meal. They can be made in advance and kept in the freezer until required.

NUTRITIONAL INFORMATION

Calories 364	Sugars 27g	
Protein 11g	Fat 24g	
Carbohydrate ...27g	Saturates 14g	

 🐁 🐁 🐁

 35 MINS   🕐 0 MINS

SERVES 4

INGREDIENTS

1 tbsp vegetarian gelatine (gelozone)

6 tbsp very hot water

3 eggs, separated

90 g/3 oz/⅓ cup caster (superfine) sugar

finely grated rind and juice of 1 lemon,
   ½ lime and ½ orange

150 ml/¼ pint/⅔ cup double (heavy) cream

125 g/4½ oz/½ cup plain fromage frais

thin lemon, lime and orange slices,
   to decorate

1 Tie greaseproof paper collars around 4 individual soufflé or ramekin dishes or around 1 large (15 cm/6 inch diameter) soufflé dish.

2 Sprinkle the gelatine (gelozone) into the very hot (not boiling) water, stirring well to disperse. Leave to stand for 2–3 minutes, stirring occasionally, to give a completely clear liquid. Leave to cool for 10–15 minutes.

3 Meanwhile, whisk the egg yolks and sugar, using a hand-held electric mixer or wire whisk until very pale and light in texture. Add the rind and juice from the fruits, mixing well. Stir in the cooled gelatine (gelozone) liquid, making sure that it is thoroughly incorporated.

4 Put the cream in a large chilled bowl and whip until it holds its shape. Stir the fromage frais and then add it to the cream, mixing it in gently. Fold the cream mixture into the citrus mixture, using a large metal spoon.

5 Using a clean whisk, beat the egg whites in a clean bowl until stiff and then gently fold them into the citrus mixture, using a metal spoon.

6 Pour the mixture into the prepared dishes, almost to the top of their collars. Allow some room for the mixture to expand on freezing. Transfer the dishes to the freezer and open-freeze for about 2 hours, until frozen.

7 Remove from the freezer 10 minutes before serving. Peel away the paper collars carefully and decorate with the slices of lemon, lime and orange.

Summer Puddings

A wonderful mixture of summer fruits encased in slices of white bread which soak up all the deep red, flavoursome juices.

NUTRITIONAL INFORMATION

Calories 250	Sugars 41g	
Protein 4g	Fat 4g	
Carbohydrate ...53g	Saturates 2g	

  10 MINS   10 MINS

SERVES 6

I N G R E D I E N T S

vegetable oil or butter, for greasing

6–8 thin slices white bread, crusts removed

175 g/6 oz/¾ cup caster (superfine) sugar

300 ml/½ pint/1¼ cups water

225 g/8 oz/2 cups strawberries

500 g/1 lb 2 oz/2½ cups raspberries

175 g/6 oz/1¼ cups black-
   and/or redcurrants

175 g/6 oz/¾ cup blackberries
   or loganberries

mint sprigs, to decorate

pouring cream, to serve

1 Grease six 150 ml/¼ pint/⅔ cup moulds (molds) with butter or oil.

2 Line the moulds (molds) with the bread, cutting it so it fits snugly.

3 Place the sugar in a saucepan with the water and heat gently, stirring frequently until dissolved, then bring to the boil and boil for 2 minutes.

4 Reserve 6 large strawberries for decoration. Add half the raspberries and the rest of the fruits to the syrup, cutting the strawberries in half if large, and simmer gently for a few minutes, until

beginning to soften but still retaining their shape.

5 Spoon the fruits and some of the liquid into moulds (molds). Cover with more slices of bread. Spoon a little juice around the sides of the moulds (molds) so the bread is well soaked. Cover with a saucer and a heavy weight, leave to cool, then chill thoroughly, preferably overnight.

6 Process the remaining raspberries in a food processor or blender, or press through a non-metallic strainer. Add enough of the liquid from the fruits to give a coating consistency.

7 Turn on to serving plates and spoon the raspberry sauce over. Decorate with the mint sprigs and reserved strawberries and serve with cream.

Banana & Mango Tart

Bananas and mangoes are a great combination of colours and flavours, especially when topped with toasted coconut chips.

NUTRITIONAL INFORMATION

Calories	....	235
Protein	....	4g
Carbohydrate	...	35g

Sugars	....	17g
Fat	....	10g
Saturates	....	.5g

1¼ HOURS   5 MINS

SERVES 8

INGREDIENTS

PASTRY

20 cm/8 inch baked pastry case

FILLING

2 small ripe bananas

1 mango, sliced

3½ tbsp cornflour (cornstarch)

50 g/1¾ oz/6 tbsp demerara
   (brown crystal) sugar

300 ml/½ pint/1¼ cups soya milk

150 ml/¼ pint/⅔ cup coconut milk

1 tsp vanilla essence (extract)

toasted coconut chips, to decorate

COOK'S TIP

Coconut chips are available in some supermarkets and most health food shops. It is worth using them as they look much more attractive and are not so sweet as desiccated (shredded) coconut.

1 Slice the bananas and arrange half in the baked pastry case with half of the mango pieces.

2 Put the cornflour (cornstarch) and sugar in a saucepan and mix together. Gradually, stir in the soya and coconut milks until combined and cook over a low heat, beating until the mixture thickens.

3 Stir in the vanilla essence (extract) then pour the mixture over the fruit.

4 Top with the remaining fruit and toasted coconut chips. Chill in the refrigerator for 1 hour before serving.

Almond Trifles

Amaretti biscuits made with ground almonds, have a high fat content.
Use biscuits made from apricot kernels for a lower fat content.

NUTRITIONAL INFORMATION

Calories 241	Sugars 23g	
Protein 9g	Fat 6g	
Carbohydrate . . .35g	Saturates 2g	

 1¼ HOURS   0 MINS

SERVES 4

I N G R E D I E N T S

8 Amaretti di Saronno biscuits

4 tbsp brandy or Amaretti liqueur

225 g/8 oz raspberries

300 ml/½ pint/1¼ cups low-fat custard

300 ml/½ pint/1¼ cups low-fat natural
fromage frais (unsweetened yogurt)

1 tsp almond essence (extract)

15 g/½ oz flaked (slivered) almonds,
toasted

1 tsp cocoa powder

1 Place the biscuits in a mixing bowl and using the end of a rolling pin, carefully crush the biscuits into small pieces.

2 Divide the crushed biscuits among 4 serving glasses. Sprinkle over the brandy or liqueur and leave to stand for about 30 minutes to allow the biscuits to soften.

3 Top the layer of biscuits with a layer of raspberries, reserving a few raspberries for decoration, and spoon over enough custard to just cover.

4 Mix the fromage frais (unsweetened yogurt) with the almond essence (extract) and spoon over the custard.

Leave to chill in the refrigerator for about 30 minutes.

5 Before serving, sprinkle with toasted almonds and dust with cocoa powder.

6 Decorate the trifles with the reserved raspberries and serve at once.

VARIATION

Try this trifle with assorted summer fruits. If they are a frozen mix, use them frozen and allow them to thaw so that the juices soak into the biscuit base – it will taste delicious.

Exotic Fruit Parcels

Delicious pieces of exotic fruit are warmed through in a deliciously scented sauce to make a fabulous barbecue (grill) dessert.

NUTRITIONAL INFORMATION

Calories	43	Sugars 9g
Protein	.........2g	Fat 0.3g
Carbohydrate	....9g	Saturates 0.1g

40 MINS   20 MINS

SERVES 4

I N G R E D I E N T S

1 paw-paw (papaya)

1 mango

1 star fruit

1 tbsp grenadine

3 tbsp orange juice

single (light) cream or natural yogurt, to serve

1 Cut the paw-paw (papaya) in half, scoop out the seeds and discard them. Peel the paw-paw (papaya) and cut the flesh into thick slices.

2 Prepare the mango by cutting it lengthways in half either side of the central stone.

3 Score each mango half in a criss-cross pattern. Push each mango half inside out to separate the cubes and cut them away from the peel.

4 Using a sharp knife, thickly slice the star fruit.

5 Place all of the fruit in a bowl and mix them together.

6 Mix the grenadine and orange juice together and pour over the fruit. Leave to marinate for at least 30 minutes.

7 Divide the fruit among 4 double thickness squares of kitchen foil and gather up the edges to form a parcel that encloses the fruit.

8 Place the foil parcel on a rack set over warm coals and barbecue (grill) the fruit for 15–20 minutes.

9 Serve the fruit in the parcel, with the low-fat natural yogurt.

COOK'S TIP

Grenadine is a sweet syrup made from pomegranates. If you prefer you could use pomegranate juice instead. To extract the juice, cut the pomegranate in half and squeeze gently with a lemon squeezer – do not press too hard or the juice may become bitter.

Mocha Swirl Mousse

A combination of feather-light yet rich chocolate and coffee mousses, whipped and attractively served in serving glasses.

NUTRITIONAL INFORMATION

Calories	130	Sugars	........10g
Protein	.........5g	Fat	...........8g
Carbohydrate	....11g	Saturates	......5g

🍲 1¼ HOURS   🕐 0 MINS

SERVES 4

INGREDIENTS

1 tbsp coffee and chicory essence (extract)

2 tsp cocoa powder, plus extra for dusting

1 tsp low-fat drinking chocolate powder

150 ml/5 fl oz/⅔ cup low-fat crème fraîche, plus 4 tsp to serve

2 tsp powdered gelatine

2 tbsp boiling water

2 large egg whites

2 tbsp caster (superfine) sugar

4 chocolate coffee beans, to serve

1 Place the coffee and chicory essence (extract) in one bowl, and 2 tsp cocoa powder and the drinking chocolate in another bowl. Divide the crème fraîche between the 2 bowls and mix both well.

2 Dissolve the gelatine in the boiling water and set aside. In a grease-free bowl, whisk the egg whites and sugar until stiff and divide this evenly between the two mixtures.

3 Divide the dissolved gelatine between the 2 mixtures and, using a large metal spoon, gently fold until well mixed.

4 Spoon small amounts of the 2 mousses alternately into 4 serving glasses and swirl together gently. Chill for 1 hour or until set.

5 To serve, top each mousse with a teaspoonful of crème fraîche, a chocolate coffee bean and a light dusting of cocoa powder. Serve immediately.

COOK'S TIP

Vegetarians should not be denied this delicious chocolate dessert. Instead of gelatine use the vegetarian equivalent, gelozone, available from health-food shops. However, be sure to read the instructions on the packet first as it is prepared differently from gelatine.

Mini Florentines

Serve these biscuits (cookies) at the end of a meal with coffee, or arrange in a shallow presentation box for an attractive gift.

NUTRITIONAL INFORMATION

Calories	75	Sugars 6g
Protein	.........1g	Fat 5g
Carbohydrate	....6g	Saturates 2g

 20 MINS   20 MINS

MAKES 40

INGREDIENTS

75 g/2¾ oz/⅓ cup butter

75 g/2¾ oz/⅓ cup caster (superfine) sugar

25 g/1 oz/2 tbsp sultanas (golden raisins)
  or raisins

25 g/1 oz/2 tbsp glacé (candied)
  cherries, chopped

25 g/1 oz/2 tbsp crystallised
  ginger, chopped

25 g/1 oz sunflower seeds

100 g/3½ oz/¾ cup flaked
  (slivered) almonds

2 tbsp double (heavy) cream

175 g/6 oz dark or milk chocolate

1 Grease and flour 2 baking trays (cookie sheets) or line with baking parchment.

2 Place the butter in a small pan and heat gently until melted. Add the sugar, stir until dissolved, then bring the mixture to the boil. Remove from the heat and stir in the sultanas (golden raisins) or raisins, cherries, ginger, sunflower seeds and almonds. Mix well, then beat in the cream.

3 Place small teaspoons of the fruit and nut mixture on to the prepared baking tray (cookie sheet), allowing plenty of space for the mixture to spread. Bake in a preheated oven, at 180°C/350°F/Gas Mark 4, for 10-12 minutes or until light golden in colour.

4 Remove from the oven and, whilst still hot, use a circular biscuit (cookie) cutter to pull in the edges to form a perfect circle. Leave to cool and crispen before removing from the baking tray (cookie sheet).

5 Melt most of the chocolate and spread it on a sheet of baking parchment. When the chocolate is on the point of setting, place the biscuits (cookies) flat-side down on the chocolate and leave to harden completely.

6 Cut around the florentines and remove from the baking parchment. Spread a little more chocolate on the coated side of the florentines and use a fork to mark waves in the chocolate. Leave to set. Arrange the florentines on a plate (or in a presentation box for a gift) with alternate sides facing upwards. Keep cool.

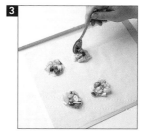

Chocolate Zabaglione

As this recipe only uses a little chocolate, choose one with a minimum of 70 per cent cocoa solids for a good flavour.

NUTRITIONAL INFORMATION

Calories . . . . . . .224 Sugars 23g

Protein . . . . .4g Fat 10g

Carbohydrate . . .23g Saturates 4g

 10 MINS   5 MINS

SERVES 4

I N G R E D I E N T S

4 egg yolks

50 g/1¾ oz/4 tbsp caster (superfine) sugar

50 g/1¾ oz dark chocolate

125 ml/4 fl oz/1 cup Marsala wine

cocoa powder, to dust

1 In a large glass mixing bowl, whisk together the egg yolks and caster (superfine) sugar until you have a very pale mixture, using electric beaters.

2 Grate the chocolate finely and fold into the egg mixture.

3 Fold the Marsala wine into the chocolate mixture.

4 Place the mixing bowl over a saucepan of gently simmering water

and set the beaters on the lowest speed or swop to a balloon whisk. Cook gently, whisking continuously until the mixture thickens; take care not to overcook or the mixture will curdle.

5 Spoon the hot mixture into warmed individual glass dishes or coffee cups (as here) and dust with cocoa powder. Serve the zabaglione as soon as possible so that it is warm, light and fluffy.

COOK'S TIP

Make the dessert just before serving as it will separate if left to stand. If it begins to curdle, remove it from the heat immediately and place it in a bowl of cold water to stop the cooking. Whisk furiously until the mixture comes together.

Apple Fritters

These apple fritters are coated in a light, spiced batter and deep-fried until crisp and golden. Serve warm with an unusual almond sauce.

NUTRITIONAL INFORMATION

Calories 438	Sugars 15g
Protein 6g	Fat 32g
Carbohydrate ...35g	Saturates 4g

 15 MINS   15 MINS

SERVES 4

INGREDIENTS

100 g/3½ oz/¾ cup plain (all-
    purpose) flour

pinch of salt

½ tsp ground cinnamon

175 ml/6 fl oz/¾ cup warm water

4 tsp vegetable oil

2 egg whites

2 eating apples, peeled

vegetable or sunflower oil,
    for deep-frying

caster (superfine) sugar and cinnamon,
    to decorate

SAUCE

150 ml/¼ pint/⅔ cup natural
    (unsweetened) yogurt

½ tsp almond essence (extract)

2 tsp clear honey

1 Sift the flour and salt together into a large mixing bowl.

2 Add the cinnamon and mix well. Stir in the warm water and vegetable oil to make a smooth batter.

3 Whisk the egg whites until stiff peaks form and fold into the batter.

4 Using a sharp knife, cut the apples into chunks and dip the pieces of apple into the batter to coat.

5 Heat the oil for deep-frying to 180°C/350°F or until a cube of bread browns in 30 seconds. Fry the apple pieces, in batches if necessary, for about 3–4 minutes until light golden brown and puffy.

6 Remove the apple fritters from the oil with a slotted spoon and drain on kitchen paper (paper towels).

7 Mix together the caster (superfine) sugar and cinnamon and sprinkle over the fritters.

8 Mix the sauce ingredients in a serving bowl and serve with the fritters.

Pistachio Dessert

An attractive-looking dessert, especially when decorated with varq, this is another dish that can be prepared in advance.

NUTRITIONAL INFORMATION

Calories 676	Sugars 98g	
Protein 15g	Fat 27g	
Carbohydrate ...98g	Saturates 9g	

15 MINS   10 MINS

SERVES 6

INGREDIENTS

850 ml/1½ pints/3¾ cups water

225 g/8 oz/2 cups pistachio nuts

225 g/8 oz/1¾ cups full-cream dried milk

500 g/1 lb 2 oz/2⅓ cups sugar

2 cardamoms, with seeds crushed

2 tbsp rosewater

a few strands of saffron

TO DECORATE

25 g/1 oz/¼ cup flaked (slivered) almonds

mint leaves

1 Put about 1 pint/600 ml/2½ cups water in a saucepan and bring to the boil. Remove the pan from the heat and soak the pistachios in this water for about 5 minutes. Drain the pistachios thoroughly and remove the skins.

2 Process the pistachios in a food processor or grind in a mortar with a pestle.

3 Add the dried milk powder to the ground pistachios and mix well.

4 To make the syrup, place the remaining water and the sugar in a pan and heat gently. When the liquid begins to thicken, add the cardamom seeds, rosewater and saffron.

5 Add the syrup to the pistachio mixture and cook, stirring constantly, for about 5 minutes, until the mixture thickens. Set the mixture aside to cool slightly.

6 Once cool enough to handle, roll the mixture into balls in the palms of your hands. Decorate with the flaked (slivered) almonds and fresh mint leaves and leave to set before serving.

COOK'S TIP

It is best to buy whole pistachio nuts and grind them yourself, rather than using packets of ready-ground nuts. Freshly ground nuts have the best flavour, as grinding releases their natural oils.

Coconut Sweet

Quick and easy to make, this sweet is very similar to coconut ice. Pink food colouring may be added towards the end if desired.

NUTRITIONAL INFORMATION

Calories 338	Sugars 5g
Protein 4g	Fat 34g
Carbohydrate 5g	Saturates 26g

 1¼ HOURS   15 MINS

SERVES 6

I N G R E D I E N T S

75 g/2¾ oz/6 tbsp butter

200 g/7 oz/3 cups desiccated
   (shredded) coconut

175 ml/6 fl oz/¾ cup condensed milk

a few drops of pink food colouring (optional)

1 Place the butter in a heavy-based saucepan and melt over a low heat, stirring constantly so that the butter doesn't burn on the base of the pan.

2 Add the desiccated (shredded) coconut to the melted butter, stirring to mix.

3 Stir in the condensed milk and the pink food colouring (if using) and mix continuously for 7–10 minutes.

VARIATION

If you prefer, you could divide the coconut mixture in step 2, and add the pink food colouring to only one half of the mixture. This way, you will have an attractive combination of pink and white coconut sweets.

4 Remove the saucepan from the heat, set aside and leave the coconut mixture to cool slightly.

5 Once cool enough to handle, shape the coconut mixture into long blocks and cut into equal-sized rectangles. Leave to set for about 1 hour, then serve.

This is a Parragon Book
This edition published in 2002

Parragon
Queen Street House
4 Queen Street
Bath BA1 1HE, UK

ISBN: 0-75257-733-6 .

Printed in China

NOTE

This book uses metric and imperial measurements. Follow the same units
of measurement throughout; do not mix metric and imperial.
All spoon measurements are level: teaspoons are assumed to be 5 ml, and
tablespoons are assumed to be 15 ml. Unless otherwise stated,
milk is assumed to be full fat, eggs and individual vegetables such as potatoes
are medium, and pepper is freshly ground black pepper.

The nutritional information provided for each recipe is per serving or per person.
Optional ingredients, variations or serving suggestions have
not been included in the calculations. The times given for each recipe are an approximate
guide only because the preparation times may differ according to the techniques used by
different people and the cooking times may vary as a result of the type of oven used.

Recipes using raw or very lightly cooked eggs should be
avoided by infants, the elderly, pregnant women, convalescents,
and anyone suffering from an illness.

The publisher would like to thank
Steamer Trading Cookshop, Lewes, East Sussex, for the kind loan of props.